Poems from India

POEMS FROM # India

SELECTED BY DAISY ALDAN

Illustrated by Joseph Low

Thomas Y. Crowell Company / New York

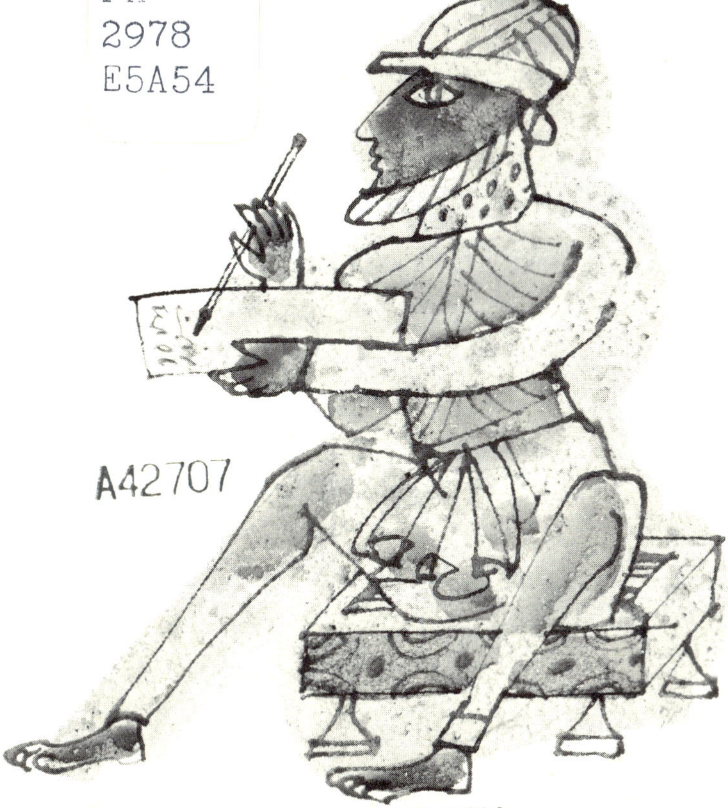

Copyright © 1969 by Daisy Aldan
Illustrations copyright © 1969 by Joseph Low

All rights reserved. Except for use in a review, the reproduction or utilization of this work in any form or by any electronic, mechanical, or other means, now known or hereafter invented, including xerography, photocopying, and recording, and in any information storage and retrieval system is forbidden without the written permission of the publisher.

Manufactured in the United States of America

L. C. Card 72-78253

1   2   3   4   5   6   7   8   9   10

ACKNOWLEDGMENTS

The editor wishes to express gratitude to the following persons for their kindness: Bonnie Crown, Susan Conheim, and Linda Hess of the Asia Society; Carol Baylin, Nissim Ezekiel, Lillian Morrison, P. Lal, Lila Ray, Marlis Schwieger, Stella Snead, and all the Indian poets and translators whose works have been included in *Poems from India*.

Grateful acknowledgment is also made to the following authors, publishers, and other copyright holders for permission to reprint the poems indicated:

THE ASIA SOCIETY for "The Washerman" by Umashankar Joshi, translated by the author, and for "Silence" by Amrita Pritam and "A Village Girl" by Mohan Singh, translated by Balwant Gargi, reprinted from *The Beloit Poetry Journal,* Winter 1962-63, Volume 13, Number 2.

SUNDERJI G. BETAI for "Roses and Thorns" by Sunderji G. Betai.

BUDDHADEVA BOSE for "The Frogs" by Buddhadeva Bose from *Modern Bengali Poems,* ed. Debrisad Chatterjee, published by The Signet Press.

Acknowledgments

AMIYA CHAKRAVARTY for "Calcutta" by Amiya Chakravarty, translated by Martin Kirkman, from *Modern Bengali Poems,* ed. Debrisad Chatterjee, published by The Signet Press.

MALAY ROY CHOUDHURY for "O K" by Malay Roy Choudhury.

THE CLARENDON PRESS, Oxford, for the translations by A. A. MacDonnell of "A Charm Against Cough," "An Imprecation Against Foes and Sorcerers," "To Secure Victory in Battle" from the *Atharva Veda* and of "The Meaning of Atman" from the *Upanishads* from *India's Past* by A. A. MacDonell.

CUNNINGHAM PRESS for "Thought" translated by F. Max Müller from the *Dhamma-pada.*

DODD, MEAD & COMPANY, INC., and WILLIAM HEINEMANN LTD for "In the Bazaars of Hyderabad" from *The Sceptered Flute* by Sarojini Naidu. Copyright 1917, 1928 by Dodd, Mead & Company, Inc.

HARVARD UNIVERSITY PRESS for the translations of Daniel H. H. Ingalls of "Villains" by Abhinanda, "Summer" by Bana, "Good Men" by Bhartrhari, "The Cremation Ground" by Bhavabhuti, "The Blossoming of Love" by Dharmakirti, "Late Winter" by Laksmidhara, "Autumn" by Manovinoda, "Darkness" by Murari, "Substantiations" by Vallana, "Epigram" by Viryamitra, "Characterization" by Yogesvara from *An Anthology of Sanskrit Court Poetry* translated by Daniel H. H. Ingalls, copyright, 1965, by the President and Fellows of Harvard College.

INDIANA UNIVERSITY PRESS for the translations by A. K. Ramanujan from the *Kuruntokai* of "What She Said" by Milaipperun Kantan, "What the Girl Said" by Kapilar, "What the Lover Said" by Allur Nanmullaiyar, "What Her Friend Said" by Varumulaiyaritti from *The Interior Landscape: Love Poems from a Classical Tamil Anthology* translated by A. K. Ramanujan, copyright © 1967 by A. K. Ramanujan; and for "Spring Wind" by Kedar Nath Agrawal, translated by L. E. Nathan, "Evening Clouds" by Dharmavir Bharati, translated by Vidya Niwas Misra and L. E. Nathan, "Since I Left the Ocean" by Navin (Balakrishna Sharma), translated by Josephine Miles, "Evening at the Seashore" by Nilan Vilochan Sharma, translated by J. Mauch, "The Family" by Visvanath, translated by Vidya Niwas Misra and Josephine Miles, from *Modern Hindi Poetry* by Vidya Niwas Misra.

Acknowledgments

KAVITA, New Delhi, for "A Snapshot" by Hem Barua from *Modern Assamese Poetry,* ed. Hem Barua; "Monologue of a Dying Man" by Jyotirmoy Datta, "A Little Girl, Rumi's Fancy" by Naresh Guha, "Follow Sleep, Fall Asleep" by Sochi Raut Roy, translated by Jyotirmoy Datta, from *Kavita International Number 100;* "Music of Stones" by Gopal Chandra Misra, "Conjecture" by Asokbijay Raha, "An Elegy for a Dead Child in the Street" by Raghavendra Rao, "Steel" by Rege from *Modern Indian Poetry,* ed. A. V. Rajeswara.

P. LAL and CALCUTTA WRITERS WORKSHOP PUBLICATIONS for "The Song of Creation," "To Agni," "To the Dawn," "To the Waters," "To the Wind" translated by P. Lal from the *Rig Veda,* from *The Golden Womb of the Sun,* copyright © 1965, by P. Lal; "The Rendezvous" by P. Lal; "Who Is the Man of Poise?" translated by P. Lal from the *Bhagavad Gita;* "All These Hurt" and "Time a River" translated by P. Lal from the *Vidyakara* by Vainateya; "The Housewife" by Balamani Amma, "The House" by Rajlukshmee Debee, "The Doves of My Eyes" by G. P. Mohanty, translated by J. M. Mohanty, "Ghazal" by Jigar Morabandi, translated by Rahm Ali Alhashmi, "Wasn't It You?" by K. R. Narasimhaswamy, translated by K. Raghavendra Rao, "The Earth Is Not an Old Woman" by Devendra Satyarthi, translated by Rahm Ali Alhasmi, reprinted from *Poetry,* January 1959, Volume 93, Number 4; "L and S" by Mahendra Kalasratha from *Calcutta Writers Workshop 3,* December, 1960.

THE LITERARY REVIEW, published by Fairleigh Dickinson University, Teaneck, New Jersey, for "The Soul of Birds" by Premendra Mitra, translated by Lila Ray.

THE MACMILLAN COMPANY for "On the Seashore" and "The Rainy Day" by Rabindranath Tagore from *The Crescent Moon* by Rabindranath Tagore, copyright 1913 by The Macmillan Company, copyright renewed 1941 by Rabindranath Tagore.

MRS. A. MARDHEKAR for "Poem" by B. S. Mardhekar, translated by Dilip Chitre, reprinted from *Poetry India.*

NEW DIRECTIONS for "The Lover's Song" and "Song of the Playing Ball" from *Shilappadikaram* by Ilango Adigal, translated by Alain Daniélou, Copyright © 1965 by Alain Daniélou.

GIEVE PATEL for "On Killing a Tree" by Gieve Patel, reprinted from "Quest."

Acknowledgments

POETRY INDIA for "The Third Continent" by Mary Erulkar, "Night of the Scorpion" by Nissim Ezekiel, "Sailing to England" by Dom Moraes, "The Stone-Breaker" by Nirala, translated by Romila Thapar, "Waves of Thought" by Pannikar, "Steel" by Rege.

QUEST, Bombay, for "The Trail" by Anil (A. R. Deshpandi), "Go at Once" by Vasant Bapat, translated by R. P. Sirkar, "Now and Then" by Sharatchandra Muktibodh, translated by D. G. Nadkarni.

TILOTTAMA RAJAN for "In Camera" by Tilottama Rajan.

LILA RAY for "A Windy Circus" from *Entrance* by Lila Ray, published by Calcutta Writers Workshop; "Cat" by Jibananda Das, translated by Lila Ray, from *Sahitya Academy Offprints,* Volume 2, Number 2; "If I Die Tomorrow" by Godwaris Mahapatra, translated by Lila Ray.

SANDHANAM PRINTING WORKS for "The White Bird" by Harindranath Chattopadhyaya.

CHARLES SCRIBNER'S SONS and CHATTO & WINDUS, LTD., for "The True and Tender Wife" from *The Ramayana* as told by Aubrey Menen. Copyright 1954 by Aubrey Menen.

NARENDRA KUMAR SETHI for "One, Two, Three" from *Song Lines of a Day* by Narendra Kumar Sethi, published by Calcutta Writers Workshop.

THE SIGNET PRESS, Calcutta, for "An Evening Air" by Samar Sen from *Modern Bengali Poems,* ed. Debiprasad Chatterjee.

R. J. SIRKAR for his translations of "Carving Away in the Mist" by Mangesh Padgaonkar, "In a Mirage I Filled My Pitcher" by Vindra Karandikar, "Then Go at Once" by Vasant Bapat.

SUNDARAM for "As a Flower I Come" by Sundaram.

KA NAA SUBRAMANYAN for "Kanya-Kumari" by Ka Naa Subramanyan.

TAPLINGER PUBLISHING COMPANY, INC., for the translations by A. L. Basham of "From *The Cloud Messenger*" by Kalidasa, "In Praise of Celibacy" from the *Sutra-krtanga,* "Radhadevi's Dance" from the *Hammira-mahakavya,* "Krishna's Longing" from the *Gita Govinda,* "A Description of Famine," "Observations" from *Naladiyar,* "Old Age" from the *Thera-gatha and Theri-gatha,* from *The Wonder That Was India* by A. L. Basham, copyright © 1968 by Taplinger Publishing Company, Inc.

POEMS OF THE WORLD
Under the editorship of Lillian Morrison

POEMS FROM FRANCE
Selected by William Jay Smith

POEMS FROM THE GERMAN
Selected by Helen Plotz

POEMS FROM INDIA
Selected by Daisy Aldan

CONTENTS

Introduction 1

POEMS OF ANCIENT INDIA 9

SANSKRIT COURT POETRY 33

OTHER POEMS OF THE MIDDLE PERIOD 43

OLD TAMIL POETRY 61

POEMS OF MODERN INDIA 73

Index of Titles 153

Index of Authors 156

Index of Translators 158

Poems from India

INTRODUCTION

India has produced a vast imaginative literature and philosophy which have enriched world culture. The *Arabian Nights, Aesop's Fables, the Decameron* stories of Boccaccio, Chaucer's *Canterbury Tales,* and some of Grimm's fairy tales probably had their origin in ancient Indian literature. Even such familiar stories as "Jack and the Beanstalk," "The Magic Mirror," and "The Seven-League Boots" have been traced to Indian sources. Spinoza, Goethe, Hegel, Emerson and Thoreau, like the other Transcendentalists and Walt Whitman, have all been influenced by the philosophy and the sacred writings of India.

The literature and religion of ancient India are inseparable, and originally almost every kind of writing, even lawbooks and grammars, was composed in the form of poetry. Yet because India has always been divided politically, racially, and linguistically, there is today no Indian poetry in the sense that there is an American, English, or French poetry. There is Bengali poetry; there is Urdu poetry, and there is poetry written in at least twelve other recognized regional languages. The one single cohesive force has been the Sanskrit language, from which developed daughter languages with their own literatures and the vernaculars spoken in India today. The great Vedas—hymns, prayers, myths, and spells addressed to the gods, from which Indian poetry developed—were recorded in the earliest known form of Sanskrit.

The Vedas are permeated with religious concern. And the Vedic poet has conveyed his devotional rapture with sublime expression and poetic skill, a marvelous gift for meter and

Introduction

metaphor. *Veda* means "wisdom" from *vid,* to know. The Vedas were supposed to have been "seen," not composed, by ancient seers.

The most ancient is the *Rig Veda,* or "Book of Psalms." The *Rig Veda* is composed of more than a thousand hymns grouped into ten books called *mandalas.* (Mandalas are mystical circles, invocations meant to accompany oblations and offerings.) The hymns are addressed to deities who are personifications of the powers of Nature. Their characteristics of power, brilliance, beneficence, and wisdom make them capable of regulating the orders of Nature and vanquishing the bringers of evil. Hindus have always been mystics whose religion has as its goal the attainment of direct union with God. The Vedas are filled with reverence, wonder, inquiry, and awakening, and one is struck by the similarity of concerns and tone to the Psalms of the Old Testament.

Religious inquiry was carried on and developed in the Upanishads, the latter portion of the Vedas. The Upanishads inquire deeply into such questions as, What is the ultimate Self? What is the spirit of the universe? What is mind? What is matter? What is God? Conclusions are discussed: Ultimate reality surpasses understanding. The individual Self within is identical with God, and by discovering this real Self, man achieves freedom and emancipation from *maya,* or illusion.

Various inquiries into many aspects of belief continued, and at the time of Buddha (c. 563–483 B.C.), there were about sixty-three contradictory schools of philosophy. Buddha presented to the world a unified, and human, philosophy. He preached a fourfold truth: that the human condition is suffering; that this suffering is caused by seeking the pleasures of the senses; that there is release from this suffering; that this release may be found in Buddha's teachings, which set forth the desirability of freeing oneself from illusions and desires. The

Introduction

Dhamma-pada, or "Words of the Doctrine," is a book of Buddhist aphorisms ascribed to the Buddha himself. It is unified in rhythm and style and theme, and infused with a high moral passion. It is a call to man to lift himself from a life of sloth, indolence, and thoughtlessness, and to strive for the knowledge and conquest of self; to free himself from lust, hatred, and anger, and to attain moral freedom.

> "Rouse thyself! Do not be idle! Follow the law of virtue! The virtuous rest in bliss in this life and the next . . ."

is the refrain.

> "If one conquer in battle a thousand times a thousand men and if another conquer himself, he is the greatest of conquerors."

It contains advice on friendship, wisdom, and folly, emphasis on self-examination, freedom from fear, moral strength and inner repose, and seems to speak directly to modern man. The concept of love toward all living things and the transformation of evil form a great part of Buddhist teaching, as they do in Christianity.

A consummation of Vedic philosophy may be found in the *Bhagavad Gita,* "Sublime Song," which forms a section of one of the two great epic masterpieces of Indian literature, The *Mahabharata,* or "The Great Bharata Story." In this and in the *Ramayana,* "The Adventures of Rama," we are brought close to the atmosphere, ideals, and customs of ancient India, and the Hindu people become real to us.

The *Mahabharata,* which is composed of a hundred thousand couplets, has often been compared with the *Iliad* of Homer, and the *Ramayana* with the *Odyssey.* Just as the subject of the *Iliad* is the Trojan war, the *Mahabharata* tells of

Introduction

the war between the dynasties of the Kurus and the Pandus. It is probable that the epic was begun about 1000 B.C., and that it assumed its present form some time before the Christian era. The main thread of the story is often interrupted by philosophical, moral, and religious discussions. At a high point of intensity in Book VI, when the rival armies confront each other before the great battle, we come upon the exquisite *Bhagavad Gita,* considered one of the greatest religious poems of all time. Questions and answers between Arjuna, noble leader of the Pandus, and Krishna, his charioteer, an incarnation of the god Vishnu, form the substance of the work. Many ethical and religious questions are discussed, and finally Krishna urges all peoples:

"Come unto me alone for refuge. I shall free thee from all sins. Grieve not."

The *Ramayana* resembles the *Odyssey* only in that it is concerned with the wanderings of Rama, son of Dasaratha, King of Ayodhya, and with his wife, Sita, who like Penelope stands the test of loyalty to her husband. The *Mahabharata* is a heroic poem that deals realistically with its characters and the depiction of violent emotion. The *Ramayana* is more tender in tone and idealistic in character portrayal. The love of Rama for his subjects, for example, is deeply touching:

"As a father to his children, to his loving men he came,
Blessed our homes and maids and matrons, 'til our infants lisped his name,
For our humble woes and troubles Rama hath a tender tear,
To our humble tales of suffering Rama lends a willing ear."

As for Sita, no woman in India is ignorant of her faithfulness and sufferings, or of her adventures in the forest and in

Introduction

prison. A higher ideal of womanly devotion and love would be hard to find.

These epics have influenced Indian life for thousands of years and remain a living reality in Indian consciousness. They bear reading in their entirety. Only excerpts from them and from other classical literary works could be included in this anthology, since most of the works of the past comprise individually a whole book or volume.

Along with the great epics, classical Sanskrit lyrical poetry reached heights of technical mastery and ingenuity. The poetry of this period was intended to produce in the reader a calm aesthetic experience—objectified grief, objectified love— which were to arise from "flavors" that the poems were said to contain. The basic human emotions—love, courage, hatred, anger, mirth, terror, pity, and surprise—formed the subject matter. Suggestion, undertone, multiplicity of meaning, were considered more important than direct statement. In the twelfth century the great scholar Vidyakara assembled the works of major classical Sanskrit poets in a comprehensive anthology. The classical Sanskrit poems that I have included, with the exception of that of Bilhana and from Kalidasa's *The Cloud Messenger,* are taken from this anthology. Kalidasa, who is sometimes called India's Shakespeare, has long been considered the master lyricist of India.

Folklore written in poetic form makes up a large and fascinating segment of Indian literature. The *Panchatantra,* a collection of animal stories, existed many years before *Aesop's Fables.* They were probably written down in Kashmir about the second century B.C., although the stories were known long before that time. In the Middle Ages the *Panchatantra* was one of the most widely translated literary works in the world.

Another great collection of poetry is the "Eight Anthologies," which represents a body of work written in Tamil, a

Introduction

South Indian language. It contains over two thousand poems, the work of two hundred poets who lived from the first to the fourth centuries after Christ.

The *Kural* by the weaver Tiruvalluvar is a collection in couplet form of 1,330 maxims. They deal with the three major aims of life—the good, the useful, and the desirable—and they present a noble human morality and worldly wisdom. The *Shilappadakaram,* "The Ankle Bracelet," a poetic drama of force and splendor, is another well-known Tamil classic.

The period from about the eleventh to the nineteenth centuries was the period of Muslim censorship and suppression, and the Indians clung for strength to traditional Sanskrit literature. With the breakdown of the Mogul Empire in the eighteenth century and the domination of the British East India Company in the early nineteenth century, European influence began to spread.

English missionaries established schools where the English language was taught. Indian families began to send their sons to England to be educated where they came into contact with the culture of the West. Indians became ashamed of their own culture, and they readily absorbed European styles and ideas. By the end of the nineteenth century, however, a new generation began to re-evaluate Indian's own heritage. The Indian National Congress was founded in 1885, and written works in Indian languages multiplied. Nevertheless, Western ideas and innovations already absorbed could hardly be annihilated, and they were incorporated in Indian literature more and more.

Rabindranath Tagore, born in Bengal in 1861, was the greatest symbol of the new spirit of Indian cultural dignity. His *Gitanjali,* "A Handful of Songs," brought him to the attention of Western readers, and in 1913 he was awarded the

Introduction

Nobel prize for literature. His poems, dramas, short stories, and philosophical writings, which reveal a lively interest in all human and earthly things and a deep spiritual insight, became world renowned.

Indian poetry in the first decades of the twentieth century tended to rely on traditional themes and techniques. The movement toward independence, which was finally achieved in 1947, brought with it a stream of socially conscious poetry. Today Indian poets have moved away from this political poetry; they seem more concerned with a personal searching, to express which they use new imagery, new forms, new vocabulary and rhythms in keeping with present experience. Like contemporary poets everywhere, they have been influenced by surrealism, German expressionism, French symbolism, T. S. Eliot, Walt Whitman, Gerard Manley Hopkins. A group that calls itself "The Hungry Generation Poets" has been influenced by the American Beats.

The contemporary poems in this volume are a sampling of the poetry in most of India's fourteen regional language groups. The ages and styles of the poets vary. Some use contemporary techniques familiar to readers in the West; others use traditional styles and themes. Some of the translations are free; others are literal; still other poems were written directly in English by poets whose first language was English before Hindi was declared the national language. In each case, what is presented is merely a taste; a complete cross-section of Indian poetry today would be impossible in one volume. There is enough evidence here, however, to show that Indian poetry today can take its place with the best of contemporary poetry anywhere. Poets are succeeding in bridging the great distances which still separate West and East, and which must be bridged if the world is to survive.

THE SONG OF CREATION

At first there was neither Being nor non-Being,
no kingdom of air, no sky beyond it.

Who straddled what, and where? Who gave shelter?
Was water there, unfathomed depth of water?

There was no death then, nor immortality,
no sign of stirring, no curtain of day or night.

Only one thing, Breath, breathed, breathing without breath,
nothing else, nothing whatsoever.

Also, there was Darkness, darkness within darkness,
the darkness of undiscriminated chaos.

Whatever existed then was void and formless.
Then came the stirring of warmth, giving shape . . .

Then rose Desire, primal Desire,
the primal seeds, the germ of Spirit.

The searching sages looked in their hearts, and knew:
Being was a manner of non-Being.

And a line cut Being from non-Being, transversely:
What was above it, what below it?

Only mighty makers, mighty forces,
action flowing freely and a fund of energy.

The Song of Creation

Who knows and who has the courage to say
he knows how the world was created?

The Primal Creator, whose eye
controls this world from highest heaven,

Whether he made this world or did not make it,
he surely knows . . . . Perhaps he also does not know.

from the *Rig Veda*
translated by P. LAL

TO THE MARUTS (The Storm Gods)

To every sacrifice you hasten together, you accept prayer after prayer, O quick Maruts! Let me therefore bring you hither by my prayers from heaven and earth, for our welfare, and for our great protection; the shakers who were born to bring food and light, self-born and self-supported, like springs, like thousandfold waves of water, aye, visibly like unto excellent bulls, those Maruts, like Soma-drops, which squeezed from ripe stems dwell, when drunk, in the hearts of the worshipper—see how on their shoulders there clings as if a clinging wife; in their hands the quoit is held and the sword. Lightly they have come down from heaven and of their own accord. Immortals, stir yourselves with the whip! The mighty Maruts on dustless paths, armed with brilliant spears, have shaken down even the strong places. O ye Maruts, who are armed with lightning-spears, who stirs you from within by himself, as the jaws are stirred by the tongue? You shake the sky, as if on the search for food; you are invoked by many, like the solar horse of the day. Where, O Maruts, is the top, where the bottom of the bottom of the mighty sky where you came? When you throw down with the thunderbolt what is strong, like brittle things, you fly across the terrible sea! As your conquest is violent, splendid, terrible, full and crushing, so, O Maruts, is your gift delightful, like the largess of a liberal worshipper, wide-spreading, laughing like heavenly lightning. From the tires of your chariot-wheels streams gush forth, when they send out the voice of the clouds; the lightnings smiled upon the earth when the Maruts showered down fatness. Prisni brought forth for the great fight the terrible train of the untiring Maruts: when fed they produced the dark cloud, and then looked about for invigorating food. May this praise, O Maruts, this song of Mandarya, the son of Mana, the poet, ask you with food for offspring for ourselves! May we have an invigorating autumn, with quickening rain!

from the *Rig Veda*

TO AGNI (God of Fire)

Scattering evil with light,
Shine on us, Agni, powerfully,
Scattering evil with light;

Our prayers are for rich fields,
For a free road and for wealth
Scattering evil with light;

We have open and excellent minds,
O Agni, thou art open and excellent,
Scattering evil with light;

Thou makest the liberal lords flourish,
Agni, thy blessings give us children,
Scattering evil with light;

O God whose arms embrace the world,
Agni, whose face shines on all sides,
Scattering evil with light;

Ferry us across the hostile waters,
O God whose face shines on all sides,
Scattering evil with light;

Ferry us from sin to goodness,
As a boatman ferries pilgrims over a stream,
Scattering evil with light.

from the *Rig Veda*
translated by P. LAL

TO THE DAWN

Young girl, shining, Dawn stirreth
    all things to life,
Maketh light, the night-hunter,
    feedeth on mortal fuel,

Foldeth bright vesture about her,
    facing the sprawling world.
Shining mother of kine, day-delighting
    colour-weaver,

Eye of the gods, gracious lady, leadeth
    her white horse to pasture:
She is dawn, lady of fastidious light,
    wealth of the world.

Come to us, Dawn, baffler of foemen,
    give full grazing pastures,
Smite those who hate us. Pour wealth
    on thy singing worshippers.

Guide us with long light,
    excellent goddess,
Give us food, grant us joy,
    and chariots, cattle, and horses.

Noble Usha, daughter of heaven,
    worshipped by the holy elders,
Grant us thy goodness,
    Bless us, goddess, now and forever.

from the Rig Veda
translated by P. L<small>AL</small>

TO THE WIND

Delighter of men's hearts
    is the wind,
a good doctor,
    a giver of long life.

Grant us life,
O wind our father!
Be to us a brother or a friend.

To your secret cave, run!
Fetch immortal honey.
Feed us, O wind!

from the Rig Veda
translated by P. LAL

TO THE WATERS

Ceaseless are the waters, ceaselessly flowing, ceaselessly cleaning, never sleeping,
Ceaselessly flowing in channels dug by Indra, the great bull, the thunderer,
Rising from the middle of the flood and flowing to their parent the sea.
    O goddess of the great waters,
    protect me.

There are waters which come from heaven, waters dug from the earth and waters gushing free
By themselves, shining waters, ceaselessly purifying, ceaselessly flowing to the ocean.
    O goddess of the great waters,
    protect me.

Presiding over the flowing waters is Varuna, who knows truth from falsehood,
Varuna, maker of holy juices, the shining one, ceaselessly purifying.
    O goddess of the great waters,
    protect me.

Varuna the king, and Soma, and the gods drink and draw strength
From the waters that ceaselessly flow, where Agni enters and resides.
    O goddess of the great waters,
    protect me.

                        from the *Rig Veda*
                        translated by P. LAL

A CHARM AGAINST COUGH

Just as the arrow sharpened well
Swift to a distance flies away,
So even thou, O cough, fly forth
Along the broad expanse of earth.

AN IMPRECATION AGAINST FOES AND SORCERERS

Avoid and pass us by, O curse,
Even as a burning fire a pond.
Here strike him down that curses us,
As Heaven's lightning strikes a tree.

TO SECURE VICTORY IN BATTLE

Arise and arm, ye spectral forms,
Followed by meteoric flames;
Ye serpents, spirits of the deep,
Demons of night, pursue our foes!

As birds start back afrighted at the falcon's cry,
As, day and night, they tremble at the lion's roar;
So thou, O drum, resound against our enemies,
Scare them away in terror, and confound their aims.

from the *Atharva Veda*
translated by A. A. MacDonnell

THE MEANING OF ATMAN

Its form can never be to sight apparent,
Not any one may with his eye behold it:
By heart and mind and soul alone they grasp it,
And those who know it thus become immortal.

Since not by speech and not by thought,
Not by the eye can it be reached:
How else may it be understood
But only when one says, 'It is'?

     from the *Upanishads*
     translated by A. A. MacDonnell

THOUGHT

As a fletcher makes straight his arrow, a wise man makes straight his trembling and unsteady thought, which is difficult to guard, difficult to hold back.

As a fish taken from his watery home and thrown on the dry ground, our thought trembles all over in order to escape the dominion of Mara, the tempter.

It is good to tame the mind, which is difficult to hold in and flighty, rushing wherever it listeth; a tamed mind brings happiness.

Let the wise man guard his thoughts, for they are difficult to perceive, very artful, and they rush wherever they list: thoughts well guarded bring happiness.

Those who bridle their mind which travels far, moves about alone, is without a body, and hides in the chamber of the heart, will be free from the bonds of Mara, the tempter.

If a man's faith is unsteady, if he does not know the true law, if his peace of mind is troubled, his knowledge will never be perfect.

If a man's thoughts are not dissipated, if his mind is not perplexed, if he has ceased to think of good or evil, then there is no fear for him while he is watchful.

Knowing that his body is fragile like a jar, and making his thought firm like a fortress, one should attack Mara, the tempter, with the weapon of knowledge; one should watch him when conquered, and should never rest.

Thought

Before long, alas! this body will lie on the earth, despised, without understanding, like a useless log.

Whatever a hater may do to a hater, or an enemy to an enemy, a wrongly directed mind will do him greater mischief.

Not a mother, not a father, will do so much, nor any other relatives; a well-directed mind will do us greater service.

from the *Dhamma-pada*
translated by F. Max Müller

OLD AGE

Black and glossy as a bee and curled was my hair;
now in old age it is just like hemp or bark-cloth.
Not otherwise is the word of the truthful . . . .

My hair clustered with flowers was like a box of sweet perfume;
now in old age it stinks like a rabbit's pelt.
Not otherwise is the word of the truthful . . . .

Dark and long-lidded, my eyes were bright and flashing as jewels;
now in old age they are dulled and dim.
Not otherwise is the word of the truthful . . . .

My voice was as sweet as the cuckoo's, who flies in the woodland thickets;
now in old age it is broken and stammering
Not otherwise is the word of the truthful . . . .

Once my hands were smooth and soft, and bright with jewels and gold;
now in old age they twist like roots.
Not otherwise is the word of the truthful . . . .

Once my body was lovely as polished gold;
now in old age it is covered all over with tiny wrinkles.
Not otherwise is the word of the truthful . . . .

Once my feet were soft, as though filled with down;
now in old age they are cracked and wizened.
Not otherwise is the word of the truthful . . . .

Old Age

Such was my body once. Now it is weary and tottering,
the home of many ills, an old house with flaking plaster.
Not otherwise is the word of the truthful.

> from the *Thera-gatha* and *Theri-gatha,*
> or "Songs of Monks and Nuns"
> translated by A. L. Basham

PRECEPTS

Enjoy the pleasure
bestowed on you,

and bear the pain
bestowed on you,

wait patiently for
what time brings,

as does the farmer
with the fruit.

~~~~~~~~~

Let us overcome
the angry man
    with gentleness,

the evil man
    with goodness,

the miser
    with generosity,

the liar
    with truth.

                         from the *Mahabharata*

ARJUNA'S PAEAN TO KRISHNA

"All the Gods do I perceive in Thy body, O God, so also the multitude of all beings. Brahma the Lord, on His Lotus-seat, all the Rishis and the Heavenly Serpent. With many arms, bodies, mouths and eyes, do I see Thee everywhere, in countless forms, neither end, middle nor beginning do I see in Thee, O Lord of everything! Thou appearest to me in all forms; Thou appearest to me with a diadem, a club, a sword, as a flaming mountain radiating out on all sides, thus do I see Thee. My vision is dazzled, as radiant fire by the brilliance of the Sun, and immeasurably great. The Everlasting, the Highest that can be known, the Greatest Good; thus dost Thou appear to me in the wide universe. The Eternal Guardian of the Eternal Right art Thou. Thou standest before my soul as the Eternal Primeval Spirit. Thou showest me no beginning, no middle and no end. Thou art eternally everywhere, infinite in force, infinite in the distance of space. Thine eyes are as big as the Moon, yea as big as the Sun itself, and out of Thy mouth there radiates sacrificial fire. I contemplate Thee in Thy glow and I perceive how Thy glow warms the universe which I can dimly sense between the ground of the Earth and the breadth of Heaven; all this is filled with Thy power. I am alone there with Thee, and that world in Heaven wherein the three worlds dwell is also within Thee, when Thy wondrous, awful Figure displays itself to my sight. I see whole multitudes of Gods coming to Thee, singing praises to Thee, and I stand there afraid, with folded hands. All the hosts of Seers call Thee blessed, and so do the multitude of Saints. They praise Thee in all their hymns of praise. The Adityas, Rudras, Vasus, Sadkyas, Visvas, Aswins, Maruts, Ushmapas, Ghandarvas, Yakshas, Siddhas, Asuras, and all the Saints praise Thee; they look up to Thee full of wonder: Such a gigantic form with so many mouths, arms, legs, feet; so many bodies, so many

Arjuna's Paean to Krishna

jaws filled with teeth; the whole world trembles before Thee, and I too tremble. The Heaven-shattering, radiating, many-armed One with a mouth working as though it were great flaming eyes, thus do I behold Thee. My soul quakes. I cannot find security or rest, O great Krishna, Who to me art Vishnu Himself. I gaze into Thy menacing innermost Being; I behold it like unto fire; I see how it works, how existence works, what is the end of all times. I gaze at Thee so, that I can know nothing of anything whatever. O! be Thou merciful unto me, Lord of Gods, Thou House in which worlds do dwell."

from the *Bhagavad Gita*

WHO IS THE MAN OF POISE?

Arjuna asked:

Who is the man of poise, Krishna?
Who is steady in devotion?
How does he speak, rest, walk?

Krishna answered:

He has shed all desire:
He is content in the Self by the Self.

He is steady. He endures sorrow.
He does not chase pleasure.
Affection, anger and fear do not touch him.

Who Is the Man of Poise?

He is not selfish.
He does not rejoice in prosperity.
He is not saddened by want.

He can recall his senses from their objects
as the tortoise pulls in its head.

Objects scatter away from the good but lazy man,
but desire remains.
In the perfect state, however, desire also goes.

Yes, this is true, for the violent senses
rock the reason of the wisest man.

But he thinks of me, the steadfast man,
commanding his desires.
His mind is stable, because his desires are subdued.

Meditation on objects breeds attachment;
from attachment springs covetousness
and covetousness breeds anger.

Anger leads to confusion,
and confusion kills the power of memory;
with the destruction of the memory choice is rendered impossible;
and when moral choice fails, man is doomed.

But a person who is established in firmness,
free from pleasure and repugnance,
traversing experience with his senses restrained—
such a person finds tranquillity.

When tranquillity comes, sorrow goes;
a person whose wisdom is tranquil is closest to Realization.

Who Is the Man of Poise?

The wavering person possesses no knowledge,
and indeed no incentive to contemplate.
There is no tranquillity for a person who will not contemplate;
and there is no bliss without tranquillity.

The mind is the ape of the wayward senses;
they destroy discrimination,
as a storm destroys boats on a lake.

The night of all beings
is the daylight of the restrained man;
and when dawn comes to all,
night has come for the perceiving sage.

The ocean, deep and silent, absorbs a thousand waters.
The saint absorbs a thousand desires,
ending in bliss which is not for the passionate.

Bliss is to be in Brahman, Arjuna,
to suffer no more delusion.
In bliss is eternal unity with Brahman,
though life itself be snuffed out.

from the Bhagavad Gita
translated by P. L<small>AL</small>

THE TRUE AND TENDER WIFE

[*Rama, banished for fourteen years by his father, King Dasaratha, bids farewell to his wife, Sita, saying he must wander alone in the pathless woods. Sita, epitome of fidelity, answers.*]

Rama spake, and soft-eyed Sita, ever sweet in speech and word,
Stirred by loving woman's passion boldly answered thus her lord:

"Do I hear my husband rightly, are these words my Rama spake,
And her banished lord and husband will the wedded wife forsake?

Lightly I dismiss the counsel which my lord hath lightly said,
For it ill beseems a warrior and my husband's princely grade!

*For the faithful woman follows where her wedded lord may lead,
In the banishment of Rama, Sita's exile is decreed,*

*Sire nor son nor loving brother rules the wedded woman's state,
With her lord she falls or rises, with her consort courts her fate.*

*If the righteous son of Raghu wends to forests dark and drear,
Sita steps before her husband wild and thorny paths to clear!*

Like the tasted refuse water cast thy timid thoughts aside,
Take me to the pathless jungle, bid me by my lord abide,

Car and steed and gilded palace vain are these to woman's life,
Dearer is her husband's shadow to the loved and loving wife!

For my mother often taught me and my father often spake
That her home the wedded woman doth beside her husband make,

As the shadow to the substance, to her lord is faithful wife,
And she parts not from her consort till she parts with fleeting life!

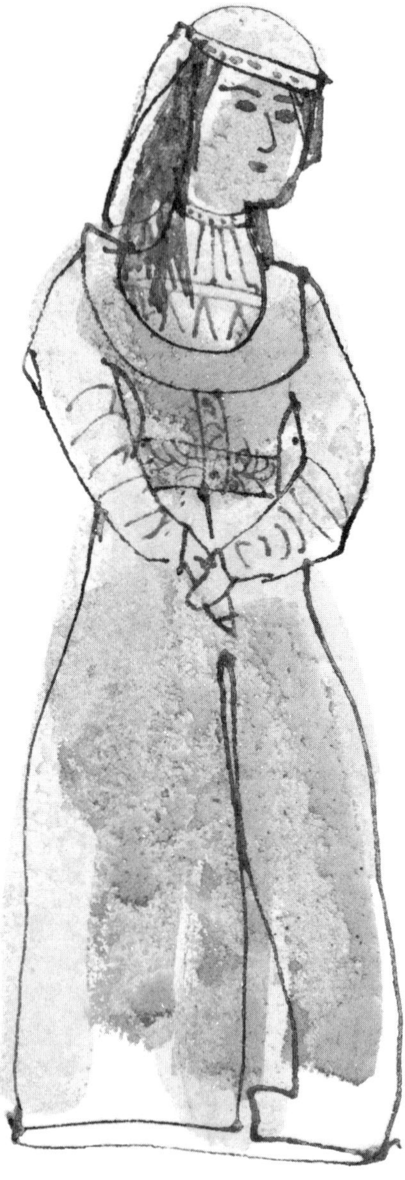

The True and Tender Wife

Therefore bid me seek the jungle and in pathless forests roam,
Where the wild deer freely ranges and the tiger makes his home,

Happier than in father's mansions in the woods will Sita rove,
Waste no thought on home or kindred, nestling in her husband's love!

World-renowned is Rama's valour, fearless by her Rama's side,
Sita will still live and wander with a faithful woman's pride,

And the wild fruit she will gather from the fresh and fragrant wood,
And the food by Rama tasted shall be Sita's cherished food!

Bid me seek the sylvan greenwoods, wooded hills and plateaus high,
Limpid rills and crystal *nullas* as they softly ripple by.

And when in the lake of lotus tuneful ducks their plumage lave,
Let me with my loving Rama skim the cool translucent wave!

Years will pass in happy union,—happiest lot to woman given,—
Sita seeks not throne or empire, nor the brighter joys of heaven.

Heaven conceals not brighter mansions in its sunny fields of pride,
Where without her lord and husband faithful Sita would reside!

Therefore let me seek the jungle where the jungle-rangers rove,
Dearer than the royal palace where I share my husband's love,

And my heart in sweet communion shall my Rama's wishes share,
And my wifely toil shall lighten Rama's load of woe and care!"

Vainly gentle Rama pleaded dangers of the jungle life,
Vainly spake of toil and trial to a true and tender wife.

from the *Ramayana* by Valmiki

Sanskrit Court Poetry

GOOD MEN

When I knew but very little
I grew mad like a rutting elephant
and in my proud heart thought
I was omniscient.
Bit by bit from consort with the wise
when I had gained somewhat of knowledge,
I knew myself a fool
and the madness left like fever.

> BHARTRHARI
> translated by DANIEL H. H. INGALLS

SUMMER

In this summer month which blasts all hope,
burns the vines, is angry at the deer,
is tree-wilting, bee-distressing, jasmine-hating,
dries up lakes, heats dust and fries the sky;
in this month that glows with cruel rays,
how can you, traveler, walk and live?

> BANA
> translated by DANIEL H. H. INGALLS

THE BLOSSOMING OF LOVE

Since congress with your mistress will be short,
like to a dream or jugglery,
and end in disillusion, stay away!
Though I reflect upon these truths a hundred times
my heart forgets not the gazelle-eyed girl.

                            DHARMAKIRTI
                       translated by Daniel H. H. Ingalls

THE CREMATION GROUND

The air is filled with faces of the torchmouth ghouls
whose mouths that open to their ears
show flaming fire and are horrible with pointed teeth,
whose hair, eyes, brows, and beard are like bright spots of lightning,
who run about, their tall cadaverous bodies
now seen, now vanishing.

> BHAVABHUTI
> translated by Daniel H. H. Ingalls

CHARACTERIZATION

How charming are the women's songs as they husk the winter rice;
a music interspersed with sound of bracelets
that knock together on round arms swinging
with the bright and smoothly rising pounder;
and accompanied by the drone of hum hum
breaking from the sharply heaving breasts.

> YOGESVARA
> translated by Daniel H. H. Ingalls

DARKNESS

The beams of heaven have been eaten
by the termites of darkness.
Through their holes now falls the sawdust
in guise of the light of stars.

                MURARI
                translated by Daniel H. H. Ingalls

AUTUMN

Now are the autumn days hospitable to wild geese,
rejuvenating medicine to fading water-lilies,
but old age for the clouds.
The rivers, now streaked with wagtails, charm the heart
with their sandbanks, rippled at the edges, rising
for the gradual lessening of the stream.

                MANOVINODA
                translated by Daniel H. H. Ingalls

VILLAINS

A friendship where one cannot act without restraint,
where one takes no joy in friendly banter
and where one friend must ever fear the other:
to such a friendship one should give wide berth.

                ABHINANDA
                translated by Daniel H. H. Ingalls

EPIGRAM

Hail, young lion, I would say a word
if you would lay aside your wrath.
By killing a full one thousand elephants,
what will your highness gain?
Do you answer, "But I am able to do thus?"
For shame, you fool! Is not the ocean
able to drown the earth, but yet refrains?

VIRYAMITRA
translated by Daniel H. H. Ingalls

SUBSTANTIATIONS

See yonder cloud
who travels to the salty sea,
endures the buffets of the winds
and is ever torn to shreds;
who still pours forth for all the earth
the water he has gained at such a price.
He does not set himself as judge of good or bad
who falls in love with charity.

                              VALLANA
                              translated by Daniel H. H. Ingalls

LATE WINTER

The monkeys shiver in the wind;
sheep, goats, and cattle, thin from cold, are suffering.
The dog, although just driven out,
returns and will not leave the oven.
And this poor man, sick with the attack of frost,
like to a turtle tries to hide
his limbs within his body.

> LAKSMIDHARA
> translated by DANIEL H. H. INGALLS

OTHER POEMS
OF THE
Middle Period

TIME A RIVER

Time a river
        flowing
its banks day and night
        falling
        crumbling

Fearfully the fallen
        clutch
and slip in the river
        flowing

Some sit calmly
        watching
others fall in the river
        flowing
of time whose banks are
        falling
daily fearfully
        crumbling.

                        VAINATEYA
                  translated by P. Lal

From *THE CLOUD MESSENGER*

[*An exile addresses a cloud to carry a message to his love from whom he is parted.*]

Stay for a while over the thickets, haunted by the girls of the hill-folk,
    then press on with faster pace, having shed your load of water,
and you'll see the Narmada River, scattered in torrents, by the rugged rocks at the foot of the Vindhyas,
    looking like the plastered pattern of stripes on the flank of an elephant.

Note by the banks the flowers of the *nipa* trees, greenish brown, with their stamens half developed,
    and the plantains, displaying their new buds.
Smell the most fragrant earth of the burnt out woodlands.
    and as you release your raindrops the deer will show you the way.

The cloud is told to visit the city of Ujjayaini . . .

Where the wind from the Sipra river prolongs the shrill melodious cry of the cranes,
    fragrant at early dawn from the scent of the opening lotus,
and, like a lover, with flattering requests,
    dispels the morning languor of women, and refreshes their limbs.

Your body will grow fat with the smoke of incense from open windows where women dress their hair.
    You will be greeted by palace peacocks, dancing to welcome you, their friend.

From *The Cloud Messenger*

If your heart is weary from travel you may pass the night above mansions fragrant with flowers,
    whose pavements are marked with red dye from the feet of lovely women.

Then the cloud will come to the magic city near the Himalayas ...

where yaksas dwell with lovely women in white mansions,
    whose crystal terraces reflect the stars like flowers.
They drink the wine of love distilled from magic trees,
    while drums beat softly, deeper than your thunder.

The Yaksa then describes his love ... and the message the cloud is to give her ...

I see your body in the sinuous creeper, your gaze in the startled eyes of deer,
    your cheek in the moon, your hair in the plumage of peacocks,
and in the tiny ripples of the river I see your sidelong glances,
    but alas, my dearest, nowhere do I find your whole likeness!

KALIDASA
translated by A. L. BASHAM

EVEN NOW ...

Even now
If my girl with lotus eyes came to me again
Weary with the dear weight of young love,
Again I would give her to these starved twins of arms
And from her mouth drink down the heavy wine,
As a reeling pirate bee in fluttered ease
Steals up the honey from the nenuphar.

Even now
When all my heavy heart is broken up,
I seem to see my prison wall breaking
And then a light, and in that light a girl,
Her fingers busied about her hair, her cool white arms
Faint rosy at the elbows, raised in the sunlight,
and temperate eyes that wander far away.

Even now
Though I am so far separate, a flight of birds
Swinging from side to side over the valley trees,
Passing my prison with their calling and crying,
Bring me to see my girl. For very bird-like
Is her song singing, and the state of a swan
Is her light walking; like the shaken wings
Of a black eagle falls her nightly hair.

Even now
I seem to see the face of my lost girl
With frightened eyes, like a wood wanderer,
In travail with sorrowful waters, unwept tears
Laboring to be born and fall; when white face turned

Even Now ...

And little ears caught at the far murmur,
The pleased snarling of the tumult of dogs
When I was hurried away down the white road.

Even now
I marvel at the bravery of love,
She, whose two feet might be held in one hand
And all her body on a shield of the guards,
Lashed like a gold panther taken in a pit
Tearfully valiant, when I too was taken;
Bearding her black-beard father in his wrath,
Striking the soldiers with white impotent hands.

Even now
I love long black eyes that caress like silk,
Ever and ever sad and laughing eyes,
Whose lids make such sweet shadow when they close
It seems another beautiful look of hers.
I love a fresh mouth, ah, a scented mouth,
And curling hair, subtle as a smoke,
And light fingers, and laughter of green gems.

Even now
She with young limbs as smooth as flower pollen,
Whose swaying body is laved in the cool
Waters of languor, this dear bright-colored bird,
Walks not, changes not, advances not
Her weary station by the black lake
Of *Gone Forever,* in whose fountain vase
Balance the water-lilies of my thought.

Even now
Death I take up as consolation.

Even Now . . .

> Nay, were I free as the condor with his wings
> Or old kings throned on violet ivory,
> Night would not come without beds of green floss
> And never a bed without my bright darling.
> It is most fit that you strike now, black guards,
> And let this fountain out before the dawn.
>
> > from *Fifty Stanzas for a Thief*
> > by Bilhana
> > translated by E. POWYS MATHERS

IN PRAISE OF CELIBACY

A celibate monk shouldn't fall in love,
    and though he hankers after pleasure he should hold himself in
        check,
for these are the pleasures
    which some monks enjoy.

If a monk breaks his vows,
    and falls for a woman,
who upbraids him and raises her foot to him,
    and kicks him on the head:

'Monk, if you won't live with me
    as husband and wife,
I'll pull out my hair and become a nun,
    for you shall not live without me!'

But when she has him in her clutches,
    it's all housework and errands!
'Fetch a knife to cut this gourd!'
    'Get me some fresh fruit!'

'We want wood to boil the greens,
    and for a fire in the evening!'
'Now paint my feet!'
    'Come massage my back!'...

'Get me my lip salve!'
    'Find my sunshade and slippers!'
'I want a knife to cut this string!'
    'Take my robe and have it dyed blue!'...

In Praise of Celibacy

'Fetch me my tweezers and my comb!'
   'Get me a ribbon to tie my hair!'
'Now pass me my looking glass!'
   'Put my toothbrush down beside me!'. . .

'Fetch the pit and the drum and the rag-ball,
   for our little boy to play with!'
'Monk, the rains are on the way,
   patch the roof of the house and look to the stores!'

'Bring me the chair with the twine seat,
   and my wooden-soled slippers to go out walking!'
So pregnant women boss their husbands,
   just as if they were household slaves.

When a child is born, the reward of their labors,
   she makes the father hold the baby.
And sometimes the fathers of sons
   stagger under their burden like camels.

They get up at night as though they were nurses,
   to lull the howling child to sleep,
and though they are shame-faced about it,
   scrub dirty garments just like washermen . . .

So, monks, resist the wiles of women,
   avoid their friendship and company.
The little pleasure you get from them
   will only lead you into trouble!

                           from the *Sutra-krtanga* of the Jains
                           translated by A. L. BASHAM

RADHADEVI'S DANCE

[*The* Hammira-mahakavya or *"Great Hammira Poem,"* *is the work of a Jain monk. The excerpt tells of Radhadevi, King Hammira's favorite dancer, who dances on the battlefield just before she is slain by a traitor.*]

In time the drummers beat their drums, the lutanists plucked
 their lutes,
the flautists blew their flutes.
Their voices in tune with the shrill flutes, the singers
sang the glory and fame of the brave Hammira . . . .
Then, the vine of her body entrancing her lovers,
awakening passion with the glance of her half-closed eyes,
to delight the hearts of the courtiers,
came Radhadevi, the dancer arrayed for the dance.

The quivering buds of her fingers moved in the dance
like tendrils of a vine, thrilling with passion . . . .
As the tips of her fingers bent, as though in a circle,
with her grace and delicate beauty all other girls seemed her slaves.
The moon, in the guise of the ring that trembled from the tip of her
 ear,
said: 'Your face is my likeness, the delusion even of sages!'
And as she danced she stirred the hearts of the young men watch-
 ing—
the hearts which lay like motes of camphor under her feet . . . .
With her gestures the necklace trembled on the tip of her breasts
like a lotus twined in the beak of a swan.
When her body bent back like a bow in the dance
like a bowstring the braid of her hair stretched down to her heel. . . .

And as she danced, at every beat of the rhythm,
she turned her back on the Saka king below.

Radhadevi's Dance

    Then in fury of soul the Lord of the Sakas spoke to his chamberlain:
'Is there any bowman who can make her his mark?'
His brother said: 'Sire, there is he whom you formerly threw into prison,
Uddanasimha—he is the only man who can do it!'
At once the Saka king had him brought, and struck off his fetters,
and arrayed the traitor finely, with double gift of affection.
And thus apparelled he took the bow which none but he could draw,
and the sinner shot her, as a hunter shoots a doe.

    At the stroke of the arrow she fainted and fell in a moat,
as lightning falls from heaven.

> from the *Hammira-mahakavya*
> by Nayacandra Suri
> translated by A. L. BASHAM

TELL ME, O SWAN

[*It is believed that Kabir, born about 1440 of Moslem ancestry, was a simple unlettered weaver who became a great religious reformer and mystical poet.*]

>Tell me, O Swan, your ancient tale.
>From what land do you come, O
>   Swan? to what shore will you
>   fly,
>Where would you take your rest, O
>   Swan, and what do you seek?
>
>Even this morning, O Swan, awake,
>   arise, follow me!
>There is a land where no doubt nor
>   sorrow have rule: where the terror
>   of Death is no more.
>There the woods of spring are a-bloom,
>   and the fragrant scent "He is I"
>   is borne on the wind:
>There the bee of the heart is deeply
>   immersed, and desires no other
>   joy.
>
>>KABIR
>>translated by RABINDRANATH TAGORE

KRISHNA'S LONGING

[*The* Gita Govinda, *or "Song of the Cowherd," of the twelfth century forms a transition from the pure lyric to the poetic drama. The subject is the love of Krishna for the beautiful Radha.*]

'Here I am dwelling. Go now to Radha,
    console her with my message, and bring her to me.'
Thus the foe of Madhu commissioned her friend,
    who went in person, and spoke to Radha thus:

'When the breeze blows from the Southern Mountains,
    and brings the Love-god with it,
when masses of flowers burst forth
    to rend the hearts of parted lovers,
he is grieved at separation from you, decked with his forest garland.

Even the cool-rayed moon inflames him,
    he is as if dead.
Struck by the arrows of love
    he complains most wretchedly.
He is grieved . . . .

When the swarming bees are murmuring
    he closes fast his ears.
His heart is clenched by parting,
    he spends his nights in fever.
He is grieved . . . .

He dwells in the depths of the forest,
    he has left his lovely home.
He tosses in sleep on the earth

Krishna's Longing

and much he murmurs your name.
He is grieved . . . .'

When the poet Jayadeva sings,
   through this pious description
of the deeds of the parted lover,
   may Hari* arise in hearts full of zeal.
He is grieved at separation from you, decked with the forest garland.

> from the *Gita Govinda,* or
> "Song of the Cowherd," by Jayadeva
> translated by A. L. BASHAM

* *Hari* is one of the names of Krishna.

ALL THESE HURT

All these hurt:
hungry children like skeletons,
heartless relatives, a leaking water pot.
But what hurts most
is my next-door neighbor's wife
with irritable indulgence lending a needle
to mend my wife's sari.

VAINATEYA
translated by P. LAL

TO WHAT SHORE WOULD YOU CROSS...

To what shore would you cross, O
 my heart? there is no traveller
 before you, there is no road:
Where is the movement, where is the
 rest, on that shore?
There is no water; no boat, no boat-
 man, is there;
There is not so much as a rope
 to tow the boat, nor a man to
 draw it.
No earth, no sky, no time, no thing,
 is there: no shore, no ford!
There, there is neither body nor mind:
 and where is the place that shall
 still the thirst of the soul? You
 shall find naught in that emptiness.
Be strong, and enter into your own
 body: for there your foothold is
 firm. Consider it well, O my heart!
 go not elsewhere.
Kabir says: "Put all imaginations
 away, and stand fast in that which
 you are."

                KABIR
             translated by RABINDRANATH TAGORE

Old Tamil Poetry

WHAT THE LOVER SAID

If one can tell morning
from noon from listless evening,
townslept night from dawn, then one's love
is a lie.
    If I should lose her
I could proclaim my misery in the streets
riding mock-horses on palmyra-stems in my wildness:
but that seems such a shame.
                 But then,
living away from her,
          living seems such a shame.

                        ALLUR NANMULLAIYAR
                        from the *Kuruntokai*
                        translated by A. K. RAMANUJAN

WHAT THE GIRL SAID

Once: if an owl hooted on the hill,
if a male ape leaped and loped
out there on the jackfruit bough in our yard
my poor heart would melt for fear. But now
               in the difficult dark of night
               nothing can stay its wandering
               on the long sloping mountain-ways
               of his coming.

                        KAPILAR
                        from the *Kuruntokai*
                        translated by A. K. RAMANUJAN

WHAT HER FRIEND SAID

He did not come just one day: he did not come just two days.
But many days he came and softened my good heart
with many modest words said many times. And
    like a honeycomb ripening on the hills
    suddenly falling
    he went.

Where is our man, good as a father, on whom we leaned?
    As from rainstorms pouring
    on a distant green land
my heart runs muddy.

                        VARUMULAIYARITTI
                        from the *Kuruntokai*
                        translated by A. K. RAMANUJAN

WHAT SHE SAID

Only the dim-witted say it's evening
    when the sun goes down,
    and the sky reddens,
    when misery deepens,
    and the mullai begins to bloom
    in the dusk.

But even when the tufted cock
    calls in the long city
    and the long night
    breaks into dawn,
    it is evening—
             even noon

is evening
    to the companionless.

                      MILAIPPERUN KANTAN
                      from the *Kuruntokai*
                      translated by A. K. Ramanujan

A GIRL SPEAKS TO HER PLAYMATE

"What bright bracelets you have! Do listen!
As I was playing in the road
he kicked over my mud castle with his foot
and snatched the garland from my head,
and ran away with my striped ball.
How he teased me, the naughty boy!

Another day my mother and I
were together, when a voice called out:
'Whoever's at home, please give me some water!'
Mother said to me: 'My dear,
fill the gilded vessel, and give him water to drink!'
I went out, not knowing who it was.
He caught my wrist, with the bangles on, and squeezed it,
and I was frightened, and cried out:
'Mother, just look what he's done!'
She was very upset, and hurried down,
but I told her he'd hiccups because of the water.
He looked at me as if he could kill me,
but then the rogue made friends with a smile."

Anonymous
translated by J. R. MARR

LOVE (To All Beings)

Is there a bolt that can avail to shut up love?
The trickling tears of loving eyes would tell it out.

The loveless to themselves belong alone:
The loving men are others' to the very bone.

Of precious Soul with body's flesh and bone
The union yields one fruit, the life of love alone.

Love maketh the heart tender towards all,
And tenderness yieldeth that priceless treasure called friendship.

Sweetness on earth and rarest bliss above,
These are the fruits of tranquil life of love.

The unwise say love avails with the virtuous alone;
Against evil too, the same is the resource.

Even as the Sun scorches the boneless worm
So does virtue the loveless one.

Life without love in its heart
Is like the withered tree in the desert sands putting forth a sprout.

Of what avail is a lovely outside,
If love, the soul's ornament, hath no place in the heart?

Bodies of loveless men are bony framework clad with skin,
Then is the body seat of life, when love resides within.

from the *Kural* by Tiruvalluvar

OBSERVATIONS

Better hatred than the friendship of fools.
    Better death than chronic illness.
Better to be killed than soul-destroying contempt.
    Better abuse than praise undeserved.

True housekeeping is to eat a meal
    sharing, as far as may be, with friend and foe alike.
The useless men who eat their food alone
    will never pass the gate of heaven.

Though you feed him with care from a golden dish
    a dog will always prefer carrion.
Though you deal with the base as you would with the good
    their deeds will always show them up.

Hillmen remember their lovely hills.
    Farmers remember their fertile fields.
The good remember another's kindness.
    The base recall only fancied slights.

As a scroll read by one who well understands it,
    as wealth to the man of generous spirit,
as a sharp sword in a warrior's hand,
    is the beauty of a faithful wife.

Observations

To those who once embraced their lovers
   whose broad chests were hung with garlands,
when their loved ones are away
   the thunder sounds like a funeral drum.

>from *Naladiyar*
>translated by A. L. BASHAM

A DESCRIPTION OF FAMINE

   The hearth has forgotten cooking:
It is overgrown with moss and mold.
The woman, thin with hunger,
Has breasts like wrinkled bladders.
Their nipples are quite dry,
But the child chews them, weeping.
She looks down at his face
And tears hang on her lashes.

>Anonymous
>translated by A. L. BASHAM

SONG OF THE PLAYING BALL

Girl, flexible as a liana,
your gold necklace tinkles in harmony
with the light girdles that confine our waists
slender as lightning-bolts.
Run! Strike the bouncing ball!
Cheer: Long live the Pândya! Long may he live!

We shall strike the bouncing ball,
and we shall sing, we shall sing:
Long life to him who wears on his broad chest
the necklace of the king of gods.
Come! Go! Sit! Dance!
—front, back, and everywhere,
as if a brilliant lightning-bolt
were falling from Heaven to Earth.

We shall strike the bouncing ball,
and we shall sing, we shall sing:
Long life to him who wears on his broad chest
the necklace of the king of gods.
The bouncing ball does not stay in the hand,
it does not fly to Heaven, it does not leave the Earth.
Come, strike the ball and sing!
Cheer: Long live the Pândya! Long may he live!

Strike the bouncing ball and sing:
Long life to him who wears on his broad chest
the necklace of the king of gods.

from *Shilappadakaram* by Ilango Adigal
translated by ALAIN DANIÉLOU

THE LOVER'S SONG

Here is the perfect picture of them all:
the Moon's become a face, with black
fish painted on it for its eyes,
a bow for brows, and clouds for hair,
in which the power of Eros hides.
Tell me, is it true that when the Moon
fled the fierce dragon that devours it in eclipse,
it found a refuge in a fisherman's hut?

These eyes are spears. See their points stained with blood,
piking some conch the sea has cast away.
For us they are the direst peril of them all.
For cruel Death, disguised as a lithe, frail girl,
has come to live here in a fishing hamlet
on the shore of the restless sea.

Look there!—a woman trying to disperse
birds crowding near her drying fish. And all
who see her feel a curious malady. She is
a lewd, fell goddess feigning a naïve village girl;
her hair is parted, modest, in five braids,
and she sits on sharp-pointed hare-leaves,
spread on the shore of the fearful sea.

from *Shilappadakaram* by Ilango Adigal
translated by ALAIN DANIÉLOU

POEMS OF
Modern India

Poems of Modern India

Assamese / Bengali / English / Gujarati
Hindi / Kannada / Malayalam / Marathi
Oriya / Panjabi / Tamil / Urdu

A SNAPSHOT

On the Indo-Pak Frontier,
near a tank,
I just chanced to see a girl,
Anamika is her name.

A snow-white *sari,* ribbons red,
hang on her body's curves in tight embrace:
I chanced to see a girl, Anamika is her name.

Beyond that embrace,
what is it that suggests itself?
Is it the freedom of the body,
or of mind?
Of minds stratified through years?
My mind, lost in the mazes of interrogations,
became a ship of the desert.

She is of the Indo-Pak Frontier,
Anamika is her name:
A whisper of spring,—a stifled voice
of noonday depth.
In every nook of my body,
there is a basket of weariness.

On the Indo-Pak Frontier,
there are bamboo groves,
a tank and a girl,—
where peace itself is a desert dream.

Across the Frontier,
there are Pakistan's men of gun,

A Snapshot

and here,
there is a girl, and I too,
unknown to her.

In their eyes,
there is a ball of fire, edg'd and violent
as booming bullets.

What a spark of fire!
What hatred! What *dispeace!*

And there's a girl,
—of eyes as of doves.
Her eyes are white wings
that buzz round a sky, hazy in smoke.

Here,
On this shore of the Frontier,
that's a living dream:
And on the other,
the devil-dance of Death.

On the Indo-Pak Frontier,
there is a girl, Anamika is her name.
Her mind's a sky,
Shimmering in purple ribbons of dreams.

On the other side of the Frontier,
bullets boom:
And on this,
there's a girl painted in a frame
of bamboo grove.

HEM BARUA
translated from Assamese by the author

CALCUTTA

Warm noon's joy spreads under the big leaved trees
Beyond the garden hedge,
The honeysuckle waves in the grey wind
On the wrought iron gate.
    And in my eyes this lovely picture goes
    With me as I fare along the lane.
    Piano-notes, unmindful on the wind
    Fill the spring sky with pain.
Along a lane in South Calcutta.

If ever I return to earth
I shall walk down this lane once more
And see the gateway in the delicate sunshine
And by its side the scarlet iris;
The closely tended flowers, the yellow and fresh blue
There, and the deep green carpet of the grass will rest my eyes.
Whose house, who lives there, these I shall not know—
But the eager pain of springtime in the farer's lonely breast,
Will fill, in the restful quiet that trembles with the piano
My eyes with joy for a passing moment.

                                AMIYA CHAKRAVARTY
                                translated from Bengali
                                by MARTIN KIRKMAN

FROGS

The rains have come, and frogs are full of glee.
They sing in chorus, with voices loud and lusty,
They sing in primeval joy:
There is nothing but fear today, neither hunger nor death.
Nor the wanton stones of fate.

Cloud-like the grasses thicken,
And in the fields the clear waters stand,
And the care-free hours of the day
Are passed in insolent singing.

In the sensual rain there is ecstasy of touch.
How luscious is the mud, how young, how soft!

They are neckless, though their throats are swollen;
They are an embodiment of the song's seventh pitch.

O what sleek bodies—cloud-like yellow and green!
Eyes staring upwards in glassy transparence,
Like the sombre stare of a mystic
Seeking God, in deep meditation.

The rain is ceased, the shadows aslant.
Hymn-like rises their singing, solemn in silent skies.

As the day pants and dies, the loud shrillness faints,
And the darkness is pierced with a sleep-begetting monophonic screech.

It is midnight. We have closed our doors and are comfortably in bed.
And the stillness is broken by a single tireless voice.

Frogs

It is the final *sloka* of the mystic chanting.
The croak, croak croak of the last lonely frog.

     BUDDHADEVA BOSE
     translated from Bengali by the author

CAT

Again and again through the day
I meet a cat.
In the tree's shade, in the sun, in the crowding brown leaves.
After the success of a few fish bones
Or inside a skeleton of white earth
I find it, as absorbed in the purring
Of its own heart as a bee.
Still it sharpens its claws on the *gulmohar* tree
And follows the sun all day long.

Now I see it and then it is gone,
Losing itself somewhere.
On an autumn evening I have watched it play,
Stroking the soft body of the saffron sun
With a white paw. Then it caught
The darkness in paws like small balls
And scattered it all over the earth.

JIBANANANDA DAS
translated from Bengali by LILA RAY

A LITTLE GIRL, RUMI'S FANCY

If I be a flower-petal,   or a little beetle,   duck,
Or a cloud of very busy,   fussy and ever busy,   bees,
Then like an erring truant,   I'll fly away, be ruined
And   leave the sums and tables,   scientific fables'   class.

Then   drop, hop. I dive,   in a blue lake I dive,   rove.
    Who could keep my track
As   daily I go and gather,   from flower and the heather   honey?
My hair though is tousled,   I am blossomed and all purpled,
Is it I who really dance on pomegranate branches,
And   though noon strikes on the clock,   father's gone to work,
It's morning here near me.

NARESH GUHA
translated from Bengali
by JYOTIRMOY DATTA

MONOLOGUE OF A DYING MAN

Here is the old fly, more eager than the rest.
They know. Although this glutton is first for the feast,
They all know I am ripe for plunder now.

For them I was born to yield them food.
Now that I think of it, what to one is living blood
Is food to the rest. In God's strange garden grow

Plants that climb upward, politicians and beans,
And those that grow beneath their toes
Could be either poets or potatoes.

What difference then between them and me?
I hear them now. So the final stillness is
Filled by beetles gnawing and, louder than beggars, the flies?

But, supposing after their banquet ends
A little is left no fly can eat,
Something invisible, secret,—

If, for your angels is left a magic residue
Which even the funeral fire fails to singe
Being lighter than air and cooler than dew!

Do as they will with my veins.
I leave them my nerve-entwined bones and those
Secret rills, if only that little remains.

Who knows but this is that alchemy
Which draws from dross a drop of purity;
This could be God's way of distilling me

Monologue of a Dying Man

From this heavy and bloated carcass of mine.
From this heap of me, he may yet extract a drop
Which, if poured into a flea, would be just enough.

To make it a fiery grain of life.
Spread like a banyan, bowed by leaf and tendril, bud and tender shoot,
All I yearn to be is a vibrant point at the tip of my root.

So the bugs be gorged and merry be their feast
For they are being used in this brewery, my body, by a gentle chemist
Squeezing from stale flesh, liquor for his lips.

JYOTIRMOY DATTA
translated from Bengali by the author

THE HOUSE

The Ancestral House talks to me. Wherever I move
The warning finger writes the 'do's' and 'don'ts.'
The 'do's' and 'don'ts' in blood that I owe
To my ancestors. This House, under the moon
Wreathes, entwines the heart with love
For what is past and half-forgotten. In a night
Of strange, dark shades, it speaks in whispering threats.

   When lights go out and face to face with the House
   I stand, the ghosts of my Ancestors rise
   To rejoice in my happiness, to console
   Me in misery. Long has been my stay
   Here, and endless memories talk today
   In every corner. When evening comes and lights
   Shine in all these rooms,—sometimes
   A fond illusion steals into my heart. I see
   Dreams take form and walk by me,
   The House as full as it used to be.

And yet, do I not hear the solitude and pain,
The dissolution of dreams, again and again?

                        RAJLUKSHMEE DEBEE
                        translated from Bengali by the author

THE SOUL OF BIRDS

Roaming the lonely wilds
I may chance upon the soul of birds.

>No longer the mere pastures.
>Neither the grains
>Nor the bare burden only.
>Now, the shining sweep,
>The rebellious flout
>That defies the world's puny pull.

In the fields and fen
They still peck at their feed
And evade nothing
Yet their heart-blood is warm
With the bluest of sky-blue oaths.

>All the qualms and clamours
>In the turns and twists of life
>Lodged deep in the heart
>>Like bullets from the hunter's gun
>Dissolve and disappear
>In that holy heat.
>Only the brave sharp swift wings
>Set no limits to the horizon

If ever this heart be utter alone
I may attain the soul of birds
Aware of another sun.

PREMENDRA MITRA
translated from Bengali
by LILA RAY

CONJECTURE

Abruptly, with a shrill crash,
The iron door breaks open.
All chains give way.

The dun bull of evening stands beside a trident.
His huge hump
Pushes up into the sky between the night and the day.
His horns hook the clouds
And beneath the heavy folds of his neck hangs a great copper gong.

Suddenly the roar of doom—
Earth splits—
Mud and the smell of jungle are everywhere.
Shadows rock with the quake.
Through the darkness the gong sounds.
Sniffing the air the bull disappears
Towards the Western hills.

      ASOKBIJAY RAHA
      translated from Bengali by LILA RAY

AN EVENING AIR

I go out in the grey evening
In the air the odor of flowers and the sounds of lamentation.

I go out into the hard loneliness of the barren field in the grey evening
In the air the odor of flowers and the sounds of lamentation.

In the gathering darkness a long, swift train suddenly
Passes me like black lightning.
Hard and ponderous and loud are the wheels.
As ponderous as the darkness, and as beautiful.

I look on, enchanted, and listen to the sounds of lamentation
In the soft fragrant air.
The long rails, grey-dark, smooth as a serpent, shiver, and

A soft, low thing cries out in the distance,
But the sounds are hard and heavy,
In the air the odor of flowers and the sounds of lamentation.

            SAMAR SEN
            translated from Bengali by the author

UNFATHOMED PAST

Tumultuous years bring their voice to your bosom,
    Unfathomed Past!

In what dark silence do you keep it gathered, covering it under
    your brooding wings?

You move in secret like midnight hours realizing dreams;
    often have I felt your muffled steps in my blood,
        have seen your hushed countenance
            in the heart of the garrulous day.

You come to write stories of our fathers in unseen scripts
    on the pages of our destiny;

You lead back to life the unremembered
    for the shaping of new images.

Is not the restless Present itself your own visions flung up
    like planets that arise
        from the bottom of dumb night?

                      RABINDRANATH TAGORE
                      translated from Bengali by the author

ON THE SEASHORE

On the seashore of endless worlds children meet.
  The infinite sky is motionless overhead and the restless water is boisterous. On the seashore of endless worlds the children meet with shouts and dances.

  They built their houses with sand, and they play with empty shells. With withered leaves they weave their boats and smilingly float them on the vast deep. Children have their play on the seashore of worlds.

  They know not how to swim, they know not how to cast nets. Pearl-fishers dive for pearls, merchants sail in their ships, while children gather pebbles and scatter them again. They seek not for hidden treasures, they know not how to cast nets.

  The sea surges up with laughter, and pale gleams the smile of the sea-beach. Death-dealing waves sing meaningless ballads to the children, even like a mother while rocking her baby's cradle. The sea plays with children, and pale gleams the smile of the sea-beach.

  On the seashore of endless worlds children meet. Tempest roams in the pathless sky, ships are wrecked in the trackless water, death is abroad and children play. On the seashore of endless worlds is the great meeting of children.

RABINDRANATH TAGORE
translated from Bengali by the author

THE RAINY DAY

Sullen clouds are gathering fast over
         the black fringe of the forest.
O child, do not go out!
The palm trees in a row by the lake are
smiting their heads against the dismal sky;
the crows with their draggled wings are silent
on the tamarind branches, and the eastern
bank of the river is haunted by a deepening
gloom.

   Our cow is lowing loud, tied at the fence.
   O child, wait here till I bring her into the
stall.
Men have crowded into the flooded field to
catch the fishes as they escape from the over-
flowing ponds; the rain water is running in
rills through the narrow lanes like a laughing
boy who has run away from his mother to
tease her.

   Listen, someone is shouting for the boat-
man at the ford.
   O child, the daylight is dim, and the crossing
at the ferry is closed.
The sky seems to ride fast upon the madly-
rushing rain; the water in the river is loud
and impatient; women have hastened home
early from the Ganges with their filled
pitchers.

The Rainy Day

The evening lamps must be made ready.
O child, do not go out!
The road to the market is desolate, the
lane to the river is slippery. The wind is
roaring and struggling among the bamboo
branches like a wild beast tangled in a net.

RABINDRANATH TAGORE
translated from Bengali by the author

THE WHITE BIRD

A white bird flew through the pale blue air,
    A white bird flew,
How like a shot, spontaneous, rare
    Soul of the blue.
Circling in joy with flutter of wing
    It passed beyond sight:
An essence of love a-wandering
    Through an essence of light.
It almost would seem that nobody saw
    That bird but I
Fulfilling unseen some loftiest law
    Of the voiceless sky.
Nobody saw it circle and go
    Like an arrow through,
Shot like a white-fire streak from a bow
    Of a blue within blue.
Nobody noticed the way it shot
    Away and afar,
How like a miracle of God's thought
    White-aimed at a star.
Was it a pigeon, was it a dove?
    Nobody knows.
All that I know is that it was like love
    Fraught with repose,
That it was like some incense fire
    Floated and sent
Higher and higher and higher and higher
    Through the firmament.
White bird, white bird! how like a bloom's
    Spirit you were

The White Bird

Soaring this noon with your clean white plumes
        Wooing the air.
Where have you gone, ah, who can tell?
        Ringing apart
Deep in my life like a heavenly bell,
        Deep in the heart,
A musical image of mine own soul
        Silent and rare,
Speeding towards one selfsame goal
        Both of us share.

        HARINDRANATH CHATTOPADHYAYA

O K

shining bangle splinters
on the dark street
                a bare-foot dog
a shriek
flutterings of a bat's wing
                cool breeze
A newspaper office cooking words
Nothing new
nothing old
                A march this or that way
                ok   ok   ok

MALAY ROY CHOUDHURY

THE THIRD CONTINENT

Where Europe and America build their arches
The pale women lean like fountains in the wind
Between the stone images; and there
The iridescent children roll like bubbles
In the laburnum-lighted squares.

And in the long snow-candled nights
The women move in moonlight ephemerally,
Phosphorescent in jewels and the rare
Northern lights of their ice-bound hair,
Before the sun comes white-winged with gulls and flying air.

But in that third Continent, dimension of deserted towers
(Whose salt-veined seas are light arching for ever
Into shadowy light, in parabolas of perpetual glare,
Where the far ships in their solitary aureoles
Seem to lie like pearls in a hand of endless air),

There, the women walk where the winds of hunger
Lament in the black harps of their hair;
And when the prayer-pierced darkness kneels upon the land
The women walk home to their weeping doors
With poverty like a lantern in their hands.

And in strangers' hearths where the golds of gold sing
While the smell of new bread swings from the windows,
All night the women's dreams cry like mice;
And in the moon-hung orchards of sleep the children laugh
Before the apple-red and hungry mornings rise.

MARY ERULKAR

NIGHT OF THE SCORPION

I remember the night my mother
was stung by a scorpion. Ten hours
of steady rain had driven him
to crawl beneath a sack of rice.
Parting with his poison—flash
of diabolic tail in the dark room—
he risked the rain again.
The peasants came like swarms of flies
and buzzed the Name of God a hundred times
to paralyse the Evil One.
With candles and with lanterns
throwing giant scorpion shadows
on the sun-baked walls
they searched for him: he was not found.
They clicked their tongues.
With every movement that the scorpion made
his poison moved in Mother's blood, they said.
May he sit still, they said.
May the sins of your previous birth
be burned away tonight, they said.
May your suffering decrease
the misfortunes of your next birth, they said.
May the sum of evil
balanced in this unreal world
against the sum of good
become diminished by your pain.
May the poison purify your flesh
of desire, and your spirit of ambition,
they said, and they sat around
on the floor with my mother in the centre,
the peace of understanding on each face.

Night of the Scorpion

More candles, more lanterns, more neighbours,
more insects, and the endless rain.
My mother twisted through and through
groaning on a mat.
My father, sceptic, rationalist,
trying every curse and blessing,
powder, mixture, herb and hybrid.
He even poured a little paraffin
upon the bitten toe and put a match to it.
I watched the flame feeding on my mother.
I watched the holy man perform his rites
to tame the poison with an incantation.
After twenty hours
it lost its sting.

My mother only said
Thank God the scorpion picked on me
and spared my children.

NISSIM EZEKIEL

A QUESTION OF WEATHER

Not to shift with weather or with tides
Of which there are improbably too many
But to hold fast to an inner hard direction
This was his credo.

After the brilliant years at college he refused
A scholarship to Oxford, and joined
A small congenial firm of publishers.
Offered a directorship at thirty he still
Lived with his parents and saved money.

I met him again the other day. 'Snails
Move as snails and rabbits feed like rabbits.
The icicle holds fast in winter. And tides
Move with a most exact direction,' he told me bleakly
Refusing a second drink.

So now it is heartening to know that she has met him,
Confronted him with her small, winning ways,
Smiled up at him and put her hand in his hand
And softness in the flesh has won.

                      Now he must learn
Tides at full moon may have their own
Extravagance, rabbits their bacchanalia, and icicles,
Persistent through the heart of winter, still must melt
To form a warm inevitable puddle
In the triumphant sun.

                                    K. C. KATRAK

L AND S

two birds
    one gay
      one sober
flying from much beyond the horizon
alighted
in the ungreen garden of my life
twittering
chirping
on a dark and gloomy day

they sang and danced merrily
me watching quietly
and feeling
the burden of the soul
      being lifted

colours sprang up all around
flowers bloomed
and poems of joy were showered here and there

the day passed
evening came
and they flew back
by bus via kurla
some ice cream and a little tea
were all they fed

dark life
gay birds
and

                      MAHENDRA KULASRESTHA

SAILING TO ENGLAND

Fallen into a dream, I could not rise.
I am in love and long to be unhappy.
Something within me raised her from the sea:
A delicate sad face, and stones for eyes.

Something within me mumbles words and grieves
For three swept out, while inland watchers groaned,
Humped, elbows jerking in a skein of waves
Like giant women knitting. One was drowned.

He could not swim and so he had to sink
And only floated after having died,
Clutching some weeds, and tolerant of the tide:
A happy traveller on a sea of ink.

I blot his eyes: waves rustle in the breeze.
Perhaps he's thinking. The moon will rise in blood,
Trawling her whisper across the sprawling seas
To rouse him, if he thinks. But if he's dead?

He must forget his death, I'll tell him so:
'It's nearly time for lunch,' I'll tell him, 'change;
Be careful: grin a bit: avoid her eyes:
Later go settle in the upstairs lounge

And laugh as if you ground stones in your teeth,
Watching the sea: or simply sit alone:
Or choose the wise alternative to death:
A nap to while away the afternoon.'

DOM MORAES

THE RENDEZVOUS

Yes, crosswise the walk in the garden.
There is the meeting, under the flame tree.
"If it is possible, and only as a favor;
You are a breath of wind."

   In a world of footfalls
   Her silence is a lily.

Summer is a solitary rose.
Ah, the heat! She shall please summer,
Pleat it in long hair.
"It is possible, but only as a favor."

   For it is not always one asks.
   O summer! O silence! be witness.

                                         P. LAL

IN THE BAZAARS OF HYDERABAD

(To the tune of the bazaars)

What do you sell, O ye merchants?
Richly your wares are displayed.
Turbans of crimson and silver,
Tunics of purple brocade,
Mirrors with panels of amber,
Daggers with handles of jade.

What do you weigh, O ye vendors?
Saffron and lentil and rice.
What do you grind, O ye maidens?
Sandalwood, henna, and spice.
What do you call, O ye pedlars?
Chessmen and ivory dice.

What do you make, O ye goldsmiths?
Wristlet and anklet and ring,
Bells for the feet of blue pigeons,
Frail as a dragon-fly's wing,
Girdles of gold for the dancers,
Scabbards of gold for the king.

What do you cry, O ye fruitmen?
Citron, pomegranate, and plum.
What do you play, O musicians?
Cithar, sarangi, and drum.
What do you chant, O magicians?
Spells for the aeons to come.

In the Bazaars of Hyderabad

What do you weave, O ye flower-girls
With tassels of azure and red?
Crowns for the brow of a bridegroom,
Chaplets to garland his bed,
Sheets of white blossoms new-gathered
To perfume the sleep of the dead.

SAROJINI NAIDU

IN CAMERA

Against a white wall I stand
A black target trapped in
Concentric circles of my
Black and white mind.

Pinned against the opposite
Wall I am
White starkness caught in the act
Of fear.

When finally you come to shoot
This daring drama of stasis
Where will you shoot? Towards
My black shadow
Or the whiteness of my terror ?

TILOTTAMA RAJAN

ON KILLING A TREE

It takes much time to kill a tree,
Not a simple jab of the knife
Will do it. It has grown
Slowly consuming the earth,
Rising out of it, feeding

On Killing a Tree

Upon its crust, absorbing
Years of sunlight, air, water,
And out of its leperous hide
Sprouting leaves.

So hack and chop
But this alone won't do it.
Not so much pain will do it.
The bleeding bark will heal
And from close to the ground
Will rise curled green twigs,
Miniature boughs
Which if unchecked will expand again
To former size.

No,
The root has to be pulled out—
Out of the anchoring earth;
It has to be roped, tied,
And pulled out—snapped out
Or pulled out entirely,
Out from the earth-cave,
And the strength of the tree exposed,
The source, white and wet,
The most sensitive, hidden
For years inside the earth.
Then the matter
Of scorching and choking
In sun and air,
Browning, hardening,
Twisting, withering,
And then it is done.

GIEVE PATEL

AN ELEGY FOR A DEAD CHILD IN THE STREET

Again the sacred parable
   is a pebble in the mouth of the street,
the sad old story of buds blasted,
of leaves rivering in the gutters,
and of the green fingers of the sun freezing.
In the complex street of man,
where ugly engines crow in the dust,
men and women move around mirages,
goats with their sorrows dream of green hills,
donkeys carrying the burden of God suffer man,
dogs feasting on his filth snarl at him
and birds neutral like children
wind their lyrical legs around his wires of death,
the only wisdom is the slaughter of innocence.
And so my eyes have been blinded by God's cruel light!
The tender flesh of a child
is so much material for twisting and crushing,
and so you became God's sudden answer,
your limbs bleeding like slashed snakes,
your face rearranged into a crushed frog,
and your last muffled cry rooted into my night!
I shall not call you a hero,
for the heart of a hero is all junk,
and yours was a temple of jasmine!
Let me ring its silver bells,
and call you rather a wind, wagging its tail,
and breaking its inner violence against a street of man!

                              RAGHAVENDRA RAO

A WINDY CIRCUS

Colouring the tissued air
cones of spun sugar hung
in a child's excited hands.
Scented sawdust, hot popcorn,
warm, sweet, buttery smells.
The wind paused, poised, spun
a top on a juggler's nose,
pasting a popple of balloons
against a papery sky.
A somersaulting gust
tossed a tumbling bush of dust,
a burst of leaves in bouncing spots
upon the leaping leopard day.
The circus tent clowned.

Lovely ladies in tinselled tights
danced upon the surging backs
of great white galloping clouds,
and acrobats in azure swung,
flung in flashing arcs from
shining top to shining top,
above the ring of the heavens.
Off the trapeze of the breeze,
roped to the poles of the afternoon,
light dropped to the ground.
Grey elephants of darkness,
brave in their tarnished gold,
knelt and crooked their trunks,
trumpeting the end of the show.

LILA RAY

ONE, TWO, THREE

One, a shrill voice,
Two, fierce anger,
Three, smoky sound.

One and two and three:

One, culture of frustration, speaking out,
Two, champagne bottle's pop,
Three, hot ashes of red words.

All three breaking into raucous laughter.

In one, genesis of the so-called culture
In two, abuse of living breath;
In three, figure of dying aspiration.

Genesis, abuse, and figure.

NARENDRA KUMAR SETHI

ROSES AND THORNS

Come, roses, with your colour and fragrance,
My heart is a flower-vase that can contain much.

Adorn it and permeate it with your scent.
Reside here and live gloriously.

And, you thorns, you may or may not come.
None is too eagerly waiting for you.

But, are you among those
waiting to be invited?

O roses, if you cannot be without thorns,
your companions from birth,
bring them along when you come,
without hesitation or second thoughts.

I shall pick you roses with loving hands
and try to avoid the thorns.
If I do not have the cleverness,
I will, of course, get scratched,
while plucking you apart.

It matters not if I get scratched.
It does not matter for I can have
my heart's delight raving over
the colour and sweet scent.

It does not matter if there is
a scratch here, a scratch there
and scratches everywhere.

> SUNDERJI G. BETAI
> translated from Gujarati by the author

THE WASHERMAN

Strolling on the bank of the Sabarmati,
the Scientist and the Poet approached
a washerman, who in beating clothes on a stone-slab
was not aware of their august presence.

The poet said: As he is beating the clothes,
what beauty unfolds itself in the water-spray!
My heart leaps up as I behold the rainbow . . .
Ah me! Were I born a century ago
I would have been a Wordsworth.

The Scientist: Eh, before Newton
there lived not even a washerman,
who could discover this simple truth
that light as it passes through water
must split itself into seven colours?

The Poet said: Washerman? What would you
expect from them? Here's one.
Rama!—he cried to the man and asked
as he stood with his mouth agape:
Do you ever care to stop and look
rapt in joy at the rainbow
in the spray with its seven colours?

The Washerman stood aghast.
He looked to his right and left.
Why on earth such important men
should find it worthwhile to talk to him.
Mabap!* if I indulged in such antics,
my children at home would perish.

*Ma: mother; bap: father.

The Washerman

The Poet: To have a glimpse of Beauty
do spare a moment for the colours seven.
If I did that, when should I finish this heap?

And unmindful of the kindly visitors,
looking downward, he began to beat
the clothes. To save himself from the spray
the Scientist moved and mumbled:
Look! to no purpose did Newton live.
His discoveries—it is the same to this man
whether they are there or not.
The poet smiled wryly: The heart
of this man does not leap up.
In vain did Wordsworth sing.

                      UMASHANKAR JOSHI
                      translated from Gujarati by the author

AS A FLOWER I COME

I'll come as a flower to you.
A child you may be, sweet and small, playing under a tree,
I'll drop on your head with a gentle tap,
And drink the innocent wonder in your eyes;
Picking me up you will toy with me,
You may tear out my petals and scatter them to the winds,
I care not.
I'll come as a flower to you.

A maiden you may be, young and sweet, with a heart of maidenly love,
The wreath I shall be, so dear to you, for your lovely hair,
Over your ears I will sway and caress your face
And adorn your hands, all eyes on me;
You may dream as you please and forget about me.
I care not.
I'll come as a flower to you.

A youth you may be, strong and fair,
On the button of your heart I will be,
Kissing the tips of your fingers all the time;
With no thought of me your mind may wander far far away,
I care not.
Ah, you know not, it is I, the only one
To drink alone from the depths of your heart.
I'll come as a flower to you.

A man you may be, glorious and great,
Then a garland I will be on your neck, richly fragrant,
Reaching down to your knees, too happy to swing with your every step;

As a Flower I Come

Your mind may move to decisions great of love and valour
Wherever you are, I with you, in the wide wide world.
I'll come as a flower to you.

And you might be the enlightened, the Blessed One, Superhuman,
I will rest then at your feet, a heap of jasmine sweet and white.
One with the dust of your feet
I shall load the dust with my fragrance rich,
And when your soul with the Supreme in communion sits,
I'll guard your gates, a guardian pure white,
Armed with the bow of purity.
I'll come as a flower to you.

      SUNDARAM
      translated from Gujarati by the author

EVENING CLOUDS

Caravals on the unmapped river
Hoist their sails,
Sleeves of magi,
As they glide over
Slowly.

Keels of emerald,
Decks awash
With marigolds—
Without a helmsman,
Unrigged they run,
With cargoes of coral and vermillion.

From far and near
They listing come
With rare lumber,
Sandalwood,
Blocks of camphor,
Casks of orange ochre,
Silks in bales,
Or a dream of nets
In tangled piles.

DHARMAVIR BHARATI
translated from Hindi
by VIDYA NIWAS MISRA
and L. E. NATHAN

SPRING WIND

Allow me; I'm the wind.
Spring wind; that's my name.

I am the very one
Who has toyed with the sky
For centuries, and did it
Effortlessly.

I am the one, yes I,
Who whistled harmony
To the sweet air
Of earth's first day.

I am the very one
Who drops the biting wine
(Spelled "Love") on every tongue
To keep all creatures young.

My holy books
Are good looks,
The facts of love,
And the red leaves of the heart.
Listen to me—
A lunatic
Of autonomy;
Therefore no need, no want—
I wander where I wander,
Light-headed traveller
Toward no house,
No purposes,

Spring Wind

No fantasies,
Not one hope,
No friends or enemies;
I'm where and what I please.

Whom I have just left
And where I go,
City, town,
Crowds,
Vacancy,
Ripe fields, whole lands,
I make them whirl,
I make them clap their hands.

Climbed the Mahua Tree
Spun its pearl head,
Jumped down thud,
Then climbed the Mango Tree
And shook it fanatically,
Whispered "Boo" in its ear,
And slid down and away.

Reached a field of green wheat:
O how long is the hour
In which my time was delight
Flying in circles there?

Linseed I saw, on its head
A pitcher of blue, and I shook
To knock that pitcher down
But had no luck,
So made the mustard dance.

Spring Wind

I forgot my own name
In the middle of this play;
But Lady Spring grew big
Blossoming for me.

A shy Arahar plant turned
Her back on my good works.
She was cold, but I burned
And so I pushed her at
An innocent passerby
And knocked the lady flat.

And that's why I laughed, you see,
And the four directions roared,
And the fields, splitting, shook,
And the sun whooped, and all
Creation crowed with me.

>KEDAR NATH AGRAWAL
>translated from Hindi by L. E. NATHAN

THE STONE-BREAKER

She, a stone-breaker.
On the road to Allahabad I met her:
    A stone-breaker.
Not the slightest shadow,
The cool of which she might have greeted.
Her dark body, withholding youth;
Eyes lowered. Thoughts buried in the stones she breaks.
Wielding the unwieldy hammer.
She strikes.
Before her sprawl the tree-girt mansions.
The mounting sun
On a hot day;
The blaze of the heat,
The scorching "loo,"*
The earth like cotton, seared,
With a mist of dust o'erspread.
    Yet another afternoon saw
    Her, a stone-breaker.
Looking up, she saw me,
Saw the houses,
But saw them with unseeing eyes:
Saw me
Through undefeated eyes.
I knew then
What I had never known before.
A moment later, her body trembling,
There fell a drop from her sweat-washed forehead.
Turning once more to the stones, she said,
"I,—a stone-breaker."

                NIRALA
                translated from Hindi by ROMILA THAPAR

* Loo: the dry hot wind of Northern India.

CIRCUIT THROUGH THE HILLS

The traveling is over, dear,
Over with the season of the fair.

Yes, all the older girls were married,
And all the younger, too, were married.
Each found an answer to her prayer;
Each wore the flowers in her hair;
But fairs have ended for the year.

O my mad daughter, you are harried,
And we've tried everywhere.
The answers never varied.
Your days go by, tear by tear,
But fairs have ended for the year.

THAKUR PRASAD SINGH
translated from Hindi by J. MAUCH

SINCE I LEFT THE OCEAN

A drop drew out of the ocean, toward the moon's height,
Began pulling between small finite, great infinite.

Forsook its vast source, then became
Minuscule, infinitesimal particle.
Immovable, succumbed to laws of motion,
Colored and cast by wind in shape and form,
        Left the ocean.

Rode a thundering and roaring force
Across the sky, cherished the notion
To measure space and time; this silly one
Drew away from its own immeasurable home;
        Left the ocean.

Turned vapor and globe of dew,
Sharp frost, soft rain, iota of contentment,
Moment of Catak's fulfillment. But where its depth?
It felt the press of living outside itself
        When it left the ocean.

Wandered the sky, entered the center of earth,
Watered roots of trees, nectared flowers,
Counted out endless time, up and down,
But could not for a moment forget its home.
        After it left the ocean.

Since I Left the Ocean

O deep ocean of affection, O distant moon
Of fulfillment, the vain drop now
Shatters. Existence outside self is untenable.
Come storming around me now; ages have gone
       Since I left the ocean.

               NAVIN
               (BALAKRISHNA SHARMA)
               translated from Hindi
               by JOSEPHINE MILES

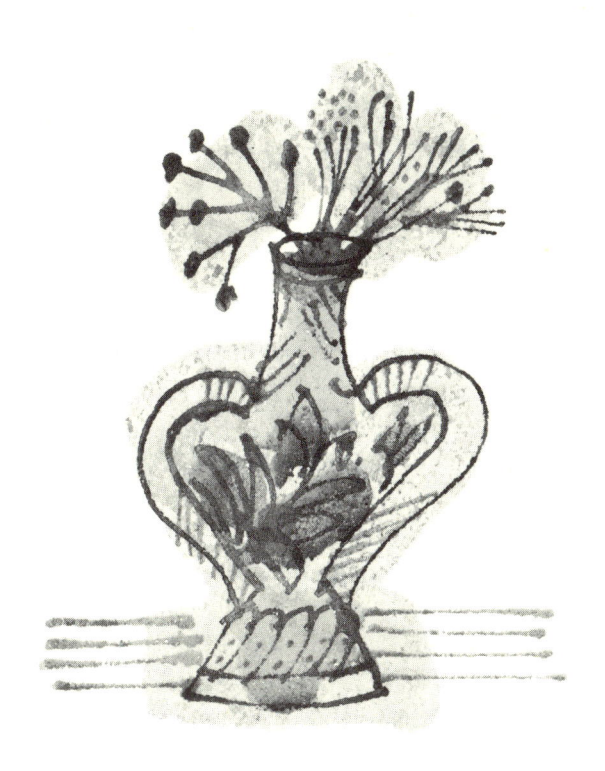

EVENING AT THE SEASHORE

Like cats, the sand dunes doze;
Waves scurry from their paws.
Clouds graze on sun's gold crop,
As confident as sheep.

A dot upon the sand,
Myself I cannot find;
For time has angled me
With boundless sky, land, and sea.

My only traces are
Thin smoke puffs in the air
And prints marking my way
That waves will snatch for play.

NALIN VILOCHAN SHARMA
translated from Hindi by J. MAUCH

THE FAMILY

My father,
   a conquered Everest,
My Mother,
   an ocean of milk poisoned by poverty.
My brother,
   a lion cub cinched up as a pack animal,
My sister,
   a doll made out of soiled clothes,
And I,
   a kettle of water
   steaming away to vapor
   water consumed into vapor.

                        VISVANATH
                        translated from Hindi
                        by VIDYA NIWAS MISRA
                        and JOSEPHINE MILES

WASN'T IT YOU?

Ten years ago, who chased me madly at the Muttur fair?
Who married me just because I lived close to his village?
    Wasn't it you?
Who roamed restlessly on the shoulders of hills and wide hillpaths?
Walked laughing, before me on the slopes and behind me in the valleys?
Who came to the door, calling me, and then asking me why I came?
Beckoned me to look, and then not to, but never forsook me?
    Wasn't it you?
The smart lad from the plains who pulled my hair?
The bold lad who held me by the sari?
The lovely boy of light who helped me cross the water of my first night?
The boy from the big house who teased me, calling me now his slave, now his pearl?
    Wasn't it you?
Who is the king of my heart, who said he was sick of me and still wanting more of me?
Who rushed down from his room when I cried as the new bangle hurt me?
Who was the hero who threatened the poor bangle-seller with a cane?
Who danced, singing, he was a river of gold and I a rain of pearls?
Wrote all kinds of things about me, called me a girl from the hills?
Gave me a new name each moment, called me moon's daughter, the moon-faced one?
    Wasn't it you?
While fixing a jasmine wreath in my hair, who brushed his lips against mine?

Wasn't It You?

Who is my sovereign, rich or poor, in joy or sorrow,—always?
    Isn't it you?
Who is your journey's companion, your wife, your child's guide?
    Look at me.

                        K. R. NARASIMHASWAMY
                        translated from Kannada by
                        K. RAGHAVENDRA RAO

THE HOUSEWIFE

When I hasten homewards after the morning bath in the river, my path resounds with the song of them that soar in the sky;
There flutter before me the green flags unfurled by those who people the nether regions;
And around me dance the butterflies, swinging their multicoloured robes.
This world, richly adorned, invites me to a glimpse of its magnificent carnival.
But mine eyes are drunk with the beauty of my home, laburnum-garlanded by the all-beholding sun.

When I hurry to my beloved, having quickly gone through the housework, the sun shines more and more in the unclouded heart of sky;
The hidden emotions of darkest depths emerge as burning sighs;
And gold-mohar shrubs, their faces marked with the auspicious saffron beaming with joy, stand by in silence.
The world transforms into a mirror held before me, but I am charmed into gazing at my own feelings reflected in the eyes of my beloved.

When I rush to my children playing in the courtyard, the sky becomes suffused by their milky smile changed into moonlight.
The ripples in the river echo their pattering footsteps;
And all the neighbouring homes are lit up by their untainted grace.
The world turns into a fairyland, wafted out of their enchanting selves.
And my soul is merged in their flower-like forms.

BALAMANI AMMA
translated from Malayalam by the author

WAVES OF THOUGHT

I fancied once that all places looked beautiful,
In silk bedecked and humming sweet songs,
A happy creator seemed then to have smilingly
Blessed the world and made nature a carnival for all.

My heart beat in tune
With the birds sitting on the boughs
In unknown language
Chirping playfully to each other.

The flowers in bloom
Smiled affectionately to each other
And the trees bent, heavy with fruit,
Whispered in each other's ears the news of their happiness.

Fields shining in moonlight,
Zephyrs scented with pollen:
Unending silence: and even night
Talked pleasantly to me.

      PANIKKAR
      translated from Malayalam by the author

THE TRAIL

I love the winding trail . . .
Of cobra coils and thickets dense
On hither side of the river bank
I love the winding trail . . .

I love the winding trail . . .
Of slip-and-slip and stuck-in-feet
Of still-wet-mud and lagging water
I love the winding trail . . .

I love the winding trail . . .
Of will-o'-the-wisps and traps and ruse
Of full-grown sags and bamboo woods
I love the winding trail . . .

I love the winding trail . . .
Of squeezings-in and ups and downs
Of tops of ghats and far beyond
I love the winding trail . . .

I love the winding trail . . .
Of hither and thither and some time whither
Sky line bound, of further on and far ahead
I love the winding trail . . .

                        ANIL (A. R. DESHPANDI)
                        translated from Marathi by the author

THEN GO AT ONCE

You will go? Then go at once.
Do not, lingering like the sweet night, pluck at my heart
And when you come again
Forget your tiny watch, forget the moments' cage.
Forget your deft touch at making up
Your urban code of neat crease and tidiness forget
Forget the string of flowers in your braided hair
Forget exquisite silken lace, forget the tinkling bracelet
Forget, dear, your speech of speed,
Forget, forget, the words of urging time-quick,
   swift, in haste, at once.
Forget the dusk and lamps lighting,
Come like the polar night's sweet mystic covering wing.
Like a calm wave of the sea,
Come tremulous, eager, heart unspoken,
   soft-intoxicate, with gentle pace.

                VASANT BAPAT
                translated from Marathi by R. P. SIRKAR

IN A MIRAGE I FILLED MY PITCHER

In a mirage I filled my pitcher
    The water is not yet dry!
But when your arms fell round my neck,
    The pitcher tottered, the water spilled.

The dusty summer in my breast
    Melted in those drops,
In a mirage I filled my pitcher
    In it I drowned all pangs.

In it dissolved borrowed hopes,
    In it subsided haughty craft,
In a mirage I filled my pitcher
    Mirage-music in my ear!

In a mirage I bathed, still bathed,
    Of a mirage I drank, still drank,
In a mirage I filled my pitcher
    The water's not yet dry.

            VINDRA KARANDIKAR
            translated from Marathi by R. P. SIRKAR

POEM

Gathering the strength
Of moment after moment
In its wrists
Memory
Plucks petals;
Unravelling knots
Of water within water
Innumerable
Shadows are seen
In the pool.

Heaven blossoms
In closed eyes;
Innocents sail
With a fearless boat!
Trapped fish
Gaze deep
Into the endless enigmas
Of reflections!

Chains binding the petals
Chain the ecstacy;
The plastic creation
Within reflections
Besieges the hypocrite!

>B. S. MARDHEKAR
>translated from Marathi by DILIP CHITRE

NOW AND THEN

If you can, now and then, will you remember me?
In the distant sunset
When beyond the rich foliage of the banyan
The hues of evening ending
You watch with great absorption . . .
Will you pluck
Along with my memory a tender red banyan leaf?

Life will be smooth and not worth complaining about,
There won't be a line on your face;
But will you send word to me once in a while?
I know that this reckless hurry doesn't become me,
Though the eyes be red—
The attitude of getting up as soon as it is light!
How can I tell you?
My mind knows no peace!
I cannot relax! In my very youth
There is a hungry, feverish speed in my bones:
The conjurer makes us dance according to his will!
Our faces are distorted—yet something drags,
The heat of the soul does not calm down.
Forgive me! Your love is quite inadequate
To drowse this slowly burning fire.
To this victim of speed won't you send something at least?
If nothing is left, send your indifference!
This dry heat has cracked the eyes
Let the tears roll freely in this way!

                          SHARATCHANDRA MUKTIBODH
                          translated from Marathi
                          by D. G. NADKARNI

CARVING AWAY IN THE MIST

We carve away in the mist
The tremulous secret of the mind;
Weave together from the waves
The reflections' mysterious signs.

The tender pulsing in the dew-drop
Feel tenderly into our knowing;
The intense formless enchantment
Bring in words to a blossom.

It throbs and thrills
In drops of dew, in rainbow arch,
In unfathomed night, in stars constellated,
In treasure of color in the *Bharapad*.

... Yet, felt, it remains in the feeling ...
In words only a mirroring—
The sun's orb to her breast straining
The river pines at heart without ceasing.

That secret ineffable, of the silence,
Of the very bourne of words,
Is felt, but never won—
Grasped, yet stretches into the beyond.

Still we carve away in the mist
Graving a mystery in the waves,
Sculpturing in silence
Cave-temples of words and images.

MANGESH PADGAONKAR
translated from Marathi by R. P. SIRKAR

STEEL

Stubborn on her lips
of steel
when flowers a blue Indeevara,
clear on one of its petals,
small as the needle's edge
is seen a point of blood.

That is mine.

My festival that.
Go, tell her
through all the strong and stately defences
of steel.

      REGE
      translated from Marathi by the author

IF I DIE TOMORROW

If I die tomorrow
    my quest shall come to an end.
Beneath black clouds
    as streaming rain
I shall be born again.

Of my making shall be
    the sound of rain falling
The trembling of forests on hills
    the flowing of streams.

In the petalled heart
    of buds that blossom
I shall spill the honey
    of clustering flowers
Among assembled leaves.

If I die suddenly,
    my work incomplete,
I shall conclude it as rain
    cloud-drawn from the sea.

                  GODAVARIS MAHAPATRA
                  translated from Oriya by LILA RAY

MUSIC OF STONES

You lifeless stones, at the immortal touch of the musical hands,
Of so many forgotten artists.
My little heart, loses its limit in joy,
You, the infinite gifts of hungry hearts or striving souls, in
       the first loneliness of mild melodies.

Drunk with the joy of love, man eternal, has played
   flute upon you, the stones, the only truth
      and truth eternal.
I have not seen a rose blooming, but I have seen
    striving, fatigued, cold-frozen hands,
    the blood-reddened fingers at work on stones.
I have not heard music, but I have heard you the stones,
    dumb and silent, scattering unheard music
    at this hour of spring, flowering in my heart of hearts.

On the day when lotus bloom, you the stones,
    the toils and the dreams of millions of Indians
    threw out its lovely petals,
    a challenge to the newly married bride
    or a worried moon in the western sky.
I have not loved life, but the stones of music
    in the hills and dales of India
    or across the roaring ocean, like a tired child
    on the mother's breast crying for its toys,
    you have showered blissful rains in the fertile
    fields of human frustration.
Stones, do tell me, who made you dance in the grand hall of silence?
Clouds sing, cuckoo pines for when the spring is away,
The proud moon wears the garland of stars.

Music of Stones

The green grass of earth makes a humble offering of sad music,
The rivers pour out their sorrows, and you the stones
   of Ajanta and Konarak, bless the music itself.

The hunter loves the bird in the vast span of the sky,
The peacocks of clouds color their feathers in the budding flowers
  of stars,
The ocean is silent, the river breathless,
     nature dying and fatigued,
And you the stones of India, you rise high,
     your music is music of millions which drive the evils of heart,
     keeps my love flowering.

I sit on the grass, upon the sky I gaze and hear the music of stones,
Imprisoned in its fold. I bow down to you the stones,
The artist, the eternal partner of my life,
You, like the burning ends of a last cigarette
Lost in the vast emptiness of the modern man's vista.

                    GOPAL CHANDRA MISRA
                    translated from Oriya by the author

THE DOVES OF MY EYES

The doves of my eyes rise to the sky's steel body
and they return daily—struck back—to this earth,
    this earth of yours—
where you wait lonely to snatch out
    the mystery of life
and the meaning of its death, and disease.

When the waves with their tiny palms
   pat softly the body of the old sand,
     I feel confused,
   and lose myself in the dryness
     of the noon-tide sun
   and realise in your pale body
    all my ancestors and
    their memories.

The secret feelings of grass and leaf
    you whisper,
   and of the forest, hill,
     moss, and pearl and sea,
   and of the pale moon in the
    battered clouds of the pale night
   and also of the feeling of floating
    from this shore to the other
     and dying.

Adamant is the steel body of the cloud
   and the doves of your mind daily
     return, defeated.
   And when the doves of my eyes return

>   fording all the wrongs of the sky
> time flows in a stream,
>   with all the dreams of my body
> and through all the tiredness, thirst,
>   hunger, excitement, and
>   sorrow of your body too.

The noon is lonely; the leaves do
   not fall; the breath of the
      sun is still;
the casuarina forest vanishes smoke-like
      in the sky;
I do not remember when or where—
   whether in the suburbs
   of Cuttack or Ujjayani—
the doves of my eyes pursued you.

>   G. P. MOHANTY
>   translated from Oriya by J. M. MOHANTY

FOLLOW SLEEP, FALL ASLEEP

Follow sleep then, fall asleep.
Follow the shadows on the wall.
The remembered and the forgotten, shadow them all.
Climb up the stairs with mark of dead men's feet,
The dark tower—a murderer's retreat.
    There ask the killer's bones
    If in his closed eyes living face shines.
Half-remembered are scattered skulls,
They are mirrors on which your heavy shadow falls;
And thus you find your bearings in that darkness deep.

Follow sleep, fall asleep.
Shadow those images that flit across
Images of your face reflected in the glass
    Of dead events and scattered time
The dark city where slums lie seam on seam,
    The fearful tunnel that endless is,
    And on no map charted the untrodden lane,
Only there can you have a whole verandah to yourself alone
    For none will mount the stairs to rend your peace.

Where through half-closed lattices
    Storm upon storm has pressed through centuries
    And dust on the window-sill carries
    Even till today the traces
Of how the howling winds were calmed
    In that room where dead emperors embalmed
Stand in row upon row to answer all your queries,
    Waiting with their wisdom of centuries
To tell you what even the clearest mirror does not reveal.

                        SOCHI RAUT ROY
                        translated from Oriya
                        by Jyotirmoy Datta

SILENCE

A pitcher of thoughts
Empty and sad
Lies in the niche of my courtyard
Silence sits thirsty
Running its tongue on its lips
Begging for a few water-words.

Desire dug a well in my courtyard
The days strike hammer strokes
The nights shovel blades
And years crack like stones
No water-word sparkles in the pit

The dark lonely well
Sits quiet resting its paw on its chin
Chewing the cud of
Clods of earth and bits of stones
Staring at the Silence.

AMRITA PRITAM
translated from Panjabi
by BALWANT GARGI

THE EARTH IS NOT AN OLD WOMAN

The earth is not an old woman—
O corn of wheat!
O flower turned cotton!
Earth is not old!

She has stood up again
With new robes.
This our earth
Is a cow who has given birth to a calf,
She is happy
She wants that all her milk be
Poured in the little mouth of the new-born.
She seems as if all her udders are full,
All her nerves are eager to give
As if a musical instrument is well-tuned,
For a new melody.
The earth is not old.

⁕⁕⁕⁕⁕⁕⁕⁕⁕⁕⁕⁕⁕⁕⁕⁕⁕

The milk is ever fresh.
Whenever any woman
Gives birth to a child,
The body becomes green,
As in spring there is youthfulness;
Again the breasts are full of milk
As if new color is filled
In the parting of the hair of Usha!*
Its taste is new,
The wheat is ever new,
The milk is ever fresh.

* Usha: The goddess of dawn.
  Hindu women apply vermilion powder to the central parting of the hair.

The Earth Is Not an Old Woman

The earth is not barren and old—
O corn of wheat!
O flowering cotton!
The earth is not old.

    DEVENDRA SATYARTHI
    translated from Panjabi by P. MACHWE

A VILLAGE GIRL

A bundle of grass on her head
She came, her hips swinging
Full like wine pitchers
She, the girl from my village

Pataki and mustard flowers
Like blue and yellow eyes
Peep through the green grass
Long blades of grass
Hang over her eyes
Like green tassles
A net of green dreams
Her face caught in it

She lifts her skirt up to her knees
And holds my arm to cross the Suhan River
Ankle-deep water rises to her knees, to her waist,
Her legs disappear beneath the shimmering water,
And her skirt goes up like an upturned umbrella

The water goes down her thighs, her knees, her ankles
So does her skirt
"Thank you brother," she says
Like a koel cooing from a mango grove
And leaves my arm and goes away

On the sand hill her footprints
Gleam like a prisoner's chain
She goes up the mound
Tall and slim like a sugar cane
And becomes a part of the green tree

A Village Girl

She did not look at me
I could not see her face caught in the green net
But I cannot shake off
The dust of her touch.

>MOHAN SINGH
>translated from Panjabi
>by BALWANT GARGI

KANYA-KUMARI

[*Kanya-Kumari is the name of the temple situated at Cape Comorin, the southernmost tip of India where the three seas meet.*]

Like any school-girl
With chintz blouse and red petticoat
Her darkling brows gathered
On the bright red spot
With pigtail dangling on the straight back
She stands at land's end where three seas meet
Waiting, waiting, waiting.

Marco Polo avers
And Indian legend tells again and again
The tale of a blood-red nose-ring
Or may be it was a diamond of flaming coal
Which flashed across the wild waves
And saved sea-mad mariners
From shipwreck on splintering rocks.

She the maiden
Stands unconscious
Of the mariners and the men and the women
Who offer her worship.
She recognizes none of the maidens
Who come to her devoutly desiring
Devoted Indian husbands.

If the mariners are saved
Or the maidens married
It is none of her doing.

Kanya-Kumari

She disdains all human purpose
To save or to marry or to drown.
Her stone-heart is not troubled
By such simple sanctifications.

Herself a miracle
Her concerns are unending
Black with age and oil and worship
Another Sakunthala having lost her ring in the waters
She is perhaps waiting to be recognized
By her Lord, a God not dead,
A being not stone.

Dim with the dimming smoke
Of ghee and incense and varied adulterations
Afire with desires which only stone
Can generate she disclaims
All miracles and would perhaps wish
To companion a live Lord
Behind closed doors.

She dreams perchance of
Uncharted seas waiting
For Marco Polos yet unborn.
She desires perhaps to meet
Maidens who do not desire
Worthy husbands. Dreams she perhaps
Of a sealess land with no rivers?

She waits perchance hardly
Knowing what she should wait for.
She waits perhaps for the three seas to dry

Kanya-Kumari

And for her to let the flood in
Or fan the orange flame
Which will flower from the waters in time.
She waits. She waits. She waits.

The seas are a miracle of dryness.
The murmur of waves never-ending
Is a miracle of silence.
She stands as a miracle of impatience
Secret in her soul. How can she,
Having seen so many miracles
How can she be so silent?

Mornings and evenings are flames
Quenched in the waters
Of day and night. Humble
Her dwelling beyond the pale of time
On the sands of the sea.
A darkling smile and a lost nose-ring
Are her only visibilities.

KA NAA SUBRAMANYAN
translated from Tamil by the author

GHAZAL

This question and difficulty is confounding me,
How do I not exist, and what if I do?

I know speaking is a crime in love,
But I must do just that, with suitable apologies.

I have been edified by the charm of blandishments
And wrapped up in a few flashes of the eyes.

With my eyes shut, how clever I am!
I can see my loved one is looking at me.

I am in possession of all truth and reality,
Although not God Himself, I am His reflection.

I know the jugglery of the world's hubbub,
And am charmed by the crystal of my own clarity.

My reputation in love is a witness
That I am all longing and restlessness.

Don't mind the weight of my distraction,
I am quite near, yet not readily sociable.

The whole secret of existence and non-existence is within me;
But on the plain of helplessness, I was the earliest model.

Lapse is my nature and fall my glory,
On reality's path I am my own guide.

You will not at all understand my purpose and meaning,
Don't listen to me: I am a far-off cry.

Ghazal

The dust of existence is too gross for my nature,
My life will begin only when I am dead.

Where is that music, observers of the world's scenes,
Which is not the tune that wells from within me?

Give me that cup of clear wine, O Saqui,*
That even in forgetfulness, I may not forget God.

Only Beauty is sure of me;
I have surrendered my heart; my sighs have no effect.

I did not allow even the hungry eyes to speak,
How much regard have I for the disposition of the Lovely Ones!

With the slightest deviation, from the path of dedication,
Every atom warns, "I am seeing!"

The book of love is open before me,
I do understand, but what do I do?

Time cannot annul me, however hard it tries,
If it is true that I am your own reflection.

From whatever angle I observe the world,
Everything seems to me my own reflection.

I am a silent melody-less music
Which makes every movement of the universe a dance.

With my song's conflagration, the world may not be consumed;
I am only the fire in the hearts of the pious.

* Saqui: the poet's muse, bearer of cups of wine.

Ghazal

The works of Imagination make no impact;
I am beyond the world of definitions.

You who are lost in dedication and prayer, find me!
I have lost myself, on reaching my destination.

Don't tease me, O gentle morning breeze,
My heart is full of longing and frustration.

Blot me out never from the pale of the living,
I give the faithful their nobility and pride.

This, my rambling incoherent talk, O Jigar,[†]
Proves, I am the voice of distraction.

JIGAR MORABANDI
translated from Urdu
by RAHM ALI ALHASHMI

[†] Jigar: the poet himself.

INDEX OF TITLES

All These Hurt, 58
Arjuna's Paean to Krishna (from the *Bhagavad Gita*), 25
As a Flower I Come, 112
Autumn, 38

Blossoming of Love, The, 36

Calcutta, 77
Carving Away in the Mist, 133
Cat, 80
Characterization, 37
Charm Against Cough, A (from the *Atharva Veda*), 18
Circuit Through the Hills, 119
Cloud Messenger, The (From), 46
Conjecture, 86
Cremation Ground, The, 37

Darkness, 38
Description of Famine, A, 69
Doves of My Eyes, The, 138

Earth Is Not an Old Woman, The, 142
Elegy for a Dead Child in the Street, An, 106
Epigram, 39
Evening Air, An, 87
Evening at the Seashore, 122

Evening Clouds, 114
Even Now . . . (from *Fifty Stanzas for a Thief*), 48

Family, The, 123
Follow Sleep, Fall Asleep, 140
Frogs, 78

Ghazal, 149
Girl Speaks to Her Playmate, A, 66
Good Men, 35

House, The, 84
Housewife, The, 126

If I Die Tomorrow, 135
Imprecation Against Foes and Sorcerers, An (from the *Atharva Veda*), 18
In a Mirage I Filled My Pitcher, 130
In Camera, 104
In Praise of Celibacy (from the *Sutra-krtanga*), 51
In the Bazaars of Hyderabad, 102

Kanya-Kumari, 146
Krishna's Longing (from the *Gita Govinda*), 56

Index of Titles

L and S, 99
Late Winter, 41
Little Girl, Rumi's Fancy, A, 81
Love (To All Beings) (from the *Kural*), 67
Lover's Song, The (from the *Shilappadakaram*), 71

Meaning of Atman, The (from the *Upanishads*), 19
Monologue of a Dying Man, 82
Music of Stones, 136

Night of the Scorpion, 96
Now and Then, 132

O K, 94
Observations (from *Naladiyar*), 68
Old Age (from the *Thera-gatha* and *Theri-gatha*), 22
On Killing a Tree, 104
On the Seashore, 89
One, Two, Three, 108

Poem, 131
Precepts (from the *Mahabharata*), 24

Question of Weather, A, 98

Radhadevi's Dance (from the *Hammira-mahakavya*), 53
Rainy Day, The, 90

Rendezvous, The, 101
Roses and Thorns, 109

Sailing to England, 100
Silence, 141
Since I Left the Ocean, 120
Snapshot, A, 75
Song of Creation, The (from the *Rig Veda*), 11
Song of the Playing Ball (from *Shilappadakaram*), 70
Soul of Birds, The, 85
Spring Wind, 115
Steel, 134
Stone-Breaker, The, 118
Substantiations, 40
Summer, 35

Tell Me, O Swan, 55
Then Go at Once, 129
Third Continent, The, 95
Thought (from the *Dhammapada*), 20
Time a River, 45
To Agni (God of Fire) (from the *Rig Veda*), 14
To Secure Victory in Battle (from the *Atharva Veda*), 18
To the Dawn (from the *Rig Veda*), 15
To the Maruts (The Storm God) (from the *Rig Veda*), 13
To the Waters (from the *Rig Veda*), 17

Index of Titles

To the Wind (from the *Rig Veda*), 16
To What Shore Would You Cross . . . , 59
Trail, The, 128
True and Tender Wife, The (from the *Ramayana*), 29

Unfathomed Past, 88

Village Girl, A, 144
Villains, 38

Washerman, The, 110
Wasn't It You, 124
Waves of Thought, 127
What Her Friend Said (from the *Kuruntokai*), 64
What She Said (from the *Kuruntokai*), 65
What the Girl Said (from the *Kuruntokai*), 63
What the Lover Said (from the *Kuruntokai*), 63
White Bird, The, 92
Who Is the Man of Poise (from the *Bhagavad Gita*), 26
Windy Circus, A, 107

INDEX OF AUTHORS

Abhinanda, 38
Adigal, Ilango, 70, 71
Agrawal, Kedar Nath, 115
Amma, Balamani, 126
Anil (A. R. Deshpandi), 128

Bana, 35
Bapat, Vasant, 129
Barua, Hem, 75
Betai, Sunderji G., 109
Bharati, Dharmavir, 114
Bhartrhari, 35
Bhavabhuti, 37
Bilhana, 48
Bose, Buddhadeva, 78

Chakravarty, Amiya, 77
Chattopadhyaya, Harindranath, 92
Choudhury, Malay Roy, 94

Das, Jibanananda, 80
Datta, Jyotirmoy, 82
Debee, Rajlukshmee, 84
Dharmakirti, 36

Erulkar, Mary, 95
Ezekiel, Nissim, 96

Guha, Naresh, 81

Jayadeva, 56
Joshi, Umashankar, 110

Kabir, 55, 59
Kalidasa, 46
Kantan, Milaipperun, 65
Kapilar, 63
Karandikar, Vindra, 130
Katrak, K. C., 98
Kulasrestha, Mahendra, 99

Laksmidhara, 41
Lal, P., 101

Mahapatra, Godavaris, 135
Manovinoda, 38
Mardhekar, B. S., 131
Misra, Gopal Chandra, 136
Mitra, Premendra, 85
Mohanty, G. P., 138, 139
Morabandi, Jigar, 149
Moraes, Dom, 100
Muktibodh, Sharatchandra, 132
Murari, 38

Naidu, Sarojini, 102
Nanmullaiyar, Allur, 63
Narasimhaswamy, K. R., 124
Navin (Balakrishna Sharma), 120
Nirala, 118

Index of Authors

Padgaonkar, Mangesh, 133
Panikkar, 127
Patel, Gieve, 104
Pritam, Amrita, 141

Raha, Asokbijay, 86
Rajan, Tilottama, 104
Rao, Raghavendra, 106
Ray, Lila, 107
Rege, 134
Roy, Sochi Raut, 140

Satyarthi, Devendra, 142
Sen, Samar, 87
Sethi, Narendra Kumar, 108
Sharma, Nalin Vilochan, 122

Singh, Mohan, 144
Singh, Thakur Prasad, 119
Subramanyan, Ka Naa, 146
Sundaram, 112
Suri, Nayacandra, 53

Tagore, Rabindranath, 88–90
Tiruvalluvar, 67

Vainateya, 45, 58
Vallana, 40
Valmiki, 29
Varumulaiyaritti, 64
Viryamitra, 39
Visvanath, 123

Yogesvara, 37

157

INDEX OF TRANSLATORS

Alhashmi, Rahm Ali, 149
Amma, Balamani, 126
Anil (A. R. Deshpandi), 128

Barua, Hem, 75
Basham, A. L., 22, 46, 51, 53, 56, 68, 69
Betai, Sunderji G., 109
Bose, Buddhadeva, 78

Chitre, Dilip, 131

Daniélou, Alain, 70, 71
Datta, Jyotirmoy, 81, 82, 140
Debee, Rajlukshmee, 84

Gargi, Balwant, 141, 144

Ingalls, Daniel H. H., 35–41

Joshi, Umashankar, 110

Kirkman, Martin, 77

Lal, P., 11, 14, 15, 16, 17, 26, 45, 56

MacDonnell, A. A., 18, 19

Machwe, P., 142
Mathers, E. Powys, 48
Marr, J. R., 66
Mauch, J., 119, 122
Miles, Josephine, 120, 123
Misra, Gopal Chandra, 136
Misra, Vidya Niwas, 114, 123
Mohanty, J. M., 139
Müller, F. Max, 20

Nadkarni, D. G., 132
Nathan, L. E., 114, 115

Panikkar, 127

Ramanujan, A. K., 63–65
Rao, K. Raghavendra, 124
Ray, Lila, 80, 85, 86, 135
Rege, 134

Sen, Samar, 87
Sirkar, R. P., 129, 130, 133
Subramanyan, Ka Naa, 146
Sundaram, 112

Tagore, Rabindranath, 55, 59, 88–90
Thapar, Romila, 118

ABOUT DAISY ALDAN

Indian poetry interested Daisy Aldan long before she spent several months in India giving readings of her own poetry and meeting Indian poets. Miss Aldan hopes this collection will communicate to young people her enthusiasm for Indian culture and philosophy as a background to those of the West.

Daisy Aldan's poetry has been published in individual volumes as well as in numerous anthologies and periodicals. Miss Aldan is the recipient of many honors, including the DeWitt American Lyric Poetry Award of the Poetry Society of America and the National Endowment of the Arts Poetry Prize. An experienced translator of French, German, and Spanish poetry, she is also well known as a critic and lecturer, and is a member of the executive board of the Poetry Society of America.

A native and resident of New York City, Daisy Aldan teaches creative writing, English, and speech at the High School of Art and Design. Terming herself an "incurable traveler," Miss Aldan has journeyed throughout most of Europe, crossed the Arctic Circle, and spent some time in Central America, the Orient, and of course, India.

ABOUT THE ILLUSTRATOR

Joseph Low was born in Corapolis, Pennsylvania; he attended schools in Oak Park, Illinois, and studied at the University of Illinois. Finding that he could pursue his own artistic interests by studying independently in museums and libraries, Mr. Low concentrated on the graphic arts; he taught himself the skills that he needed and acquired the necessary tools.

After spending some time at the Art Students League in New York City, Joseph Low taught graphic arts at Indiana University for three years. He is not only an artist but also a printer and publisher, with his own Eden Hill Press.

His work has been exhibited in museums across the United States, in South America, in the Orient, and in Europe. He and his wife live in Connecticut. Their house overlooks Long Island Sound and the Norwalk Islands, and is a ten-minute walk from their boat, a midget ocean racer.